I0120796

CoupleCARE

Couple Commitment
and Relationship Enhancement

W. Kim Halford

Couple Guidebook

AUSTRALIANACADEMICPRESS

Other components to the CoupleCARE Program
CoupleCARE Educator's Manual
CoupleCARE Video Guide

First published 2017 by:
Australian Academic Press Group Pty. Ltd.
18 Victor Russell Drive
Samford Valley QLD 4520, Australia
www.australianacademicpress.com.au

Disclaimer
Every effort has been made in preparing this work to provide information based on accepted standards and practice at the time of publication. The publisher, however, makes no warranties of any kind of psychological outcome relating to use of this work and disclaims all responsibility or liability for direct or consequential damages resulting from any use of the material contained in this work.

ISBN 9781922117892

Publisher: Stephen May

Cover design, page design & typesetting: Australian Academic Press

Printing: Lightning Source

Dedication

The practice of couple relationship education blends the deeply personal with professional practice. My research, my professional practice, my conversations with family and friends, and being married to Barbara for nearly 40 years, all convince me that sharing the journey with someone special is central to a healthy life. I dedicate this book to my oldest son James Halford and daughter–in-law Rocio Carmen Ponce Reyes who married during the time I worked on the second edition of this program. Their relationship is testament to what working at a relationship can achieve, I hope they will continue to cherish and love each other in a long life together.

I know people say you have to work at a relationship, but I'm really not sure how to work at it. What do I do?

Lisa, 28, engaged to be married next year.

I'm so excited about our relationship and the future. But I can't help being a bit scared too. Will it last? I really hope so.

Johann, 45, recently married for the second time.

We get on really well, we have many common interests and our personalities are similar. I think we communicate well. I think we resolve conflicts well. How can I be sure, though? And what if things change?

Mee Ling, 33, in a committed relationship for 2 years.

We only got married last year. John means so much to me. Over the past year I've learned a lot about the importance of being aware of the way I am in my relationship and some ways of improving things by actually making changes to my own behaviour. CoupleCARE triggered off lots of these ideas.

Chantelle, 49, married.

Anqi seemed to want us to spend all our weekends with her family. That seemed weird to me. After doing Couple CARE I think I get why family is so important to her. That understanding has changed me, ... for the better I think.

Mick, 57, recently married to someone from a very different cultural background.

I used to think relationships should just happen naturally. After CoupleCARE I realise there is lots to having a great relationship that you can learn.

Riyad, 31, planning for a future with his partner.

Contents

Unit 5   Sexual Intimacy

Unit 6   Looking Ahead

Acknowledgments

The CoupleCARE program was first developed and evaluated in the late 1990s by a team of psychologists led by me (Professor Kim Halford) at Griffith University, in Brisbane Australia. Very important contributions were made to the first edition of CoupleCARE, which was published in 2006, by Professor Keithia Wilson, Ms. Elizabeth Moore, Ms. Carmel Dyer and Mr. Charles Farrugia all of Griffith University.

Further work was done to refine and evaluate CoupleCARE when I moved in 2009 to the University of Queensland, which also is in Brisbane. Particularly important contributions to the second edition of CoupleCARE were made by Dr. Melissa Bakhurst, Dr. Ruth Bouma, Dr. Chris Pepping, Dr. Angie Ho, Dr. Danika Hiew, and Dr. Alice Hucker of the University of Queensland, and Dr. Jemima Petch who is Director of Research at Relationships Australia — Queensland (RAQ). The Australian Research Council and the National Health and Medical Research Council of Australia funded much of the program of research that led to the program in its current form, and we are very grateful for that support.

Further research on CoupleCARE has been done in the United States in collaboration with Professors Jeffry Larson, Dean Busby and Tom Holman of Brigham Young University. That research was supported by the RELATE Institute, which is affiliated with Brigham Young University. There is ongoing work evaluating a US adaptation of CoupleCARE being conducted in collaboration with Professors Richard Heyman and Amy Slep of New York University, which is funded by the US Center for Disease Control. In addition, there is ongoing work in Europe being done to evaluate a Swiss adaptation of CoupleCARE in collaboration with Professor Guy Bodenmann and Dr. Valentinna Anderegg of the University of Zurich, funded by the Swiss Science Foundation.

This second edition of CoupleCARE owes much to an ongoing collaboration I have with RAQ. The opportunity to work closely with their dedicated professionals to do extensive field testing of CoupleCARE has been very important in refining the current edition of CoupleCARE. RAQ also have provided considerable funding toward the costs of production of the CoupleCARE materials. I am very grateful to the RAQ Chief Executive Dr. Ian Law, his predecessor Mr. Shane Klintworth, and before him Mr. Andrew Davis, for their support of the development, evaluation and use of CoupleCARE. I also thank the RAQ Executive for their commitment to refining evidence-based practice of family services.

Mr. Peter Marshall is an independent video producer who directed the video component of the current edition of the program, and patiently guided me through the intricacies of audiovisual production.

Mr. Stephen May, Chief Executive of Australian Academic Press, has been a great editor and publisher of the first and second editions of CoupleCARE. His skilled team have done much excellent work on the design and production of the materials.

Finally, thousands of couples have entrusted the CoupleCARE team with the challenge of helping them to enhance their relationships. Some couples came as volunteers in research projects, others sought us out for help in making their relationships stronger and more loving. Their openness to working on their relationship instilled in us a fundamental optimism about improving and sustaining quality relationships.

The content of the CoupleCARE program is a collection of work by many people, and I am grateful to all of them.

Kim Halford
December 2016.

Welcome to CoupleCARE

Welcome to CoupleCARE, the Couple Commitment And Relationship Enhancement program. We are delighted that you have chosen to work with us on something so important to you — your relationship with your partner. In taking part you are making a positive step to strengthen your relationship.

A great relationship with someone you love brings the joy of sharing life's good times. It also brings mutual support in managing life's challenges. Most couple relationships start well, and the partners are happy. Many relationships stay happy, at least most of the time. Those couples that stay happy put in some effort in making their relationship work. CoupleCARE shows you how to strengthen your relationship and keep it strong and happy.

Unfortunately, quite a lot of couples that start happy do not stay that way. In Australia, North America and much of Europe about 40% to 50% of marriages end in divorce, and over 60% of all couples that live together break up. In Asian countries such as Japan and China, and in India, divorce rates are somewhat lower than in Western countries, but the trends are for increasing rates of break up. In CoupleCARE we show you how to recognise possible future problems, and how to prevent such problems.

There is no one right way to have a great relationship. So, in CoupleCARE you decide how you want your relationship to develop. At the same time, there are common challenges many couples share. In CoupleCARE we offer ideas on how to address those challenges and strengthen your relationship. In each unit you are invited to consider the ideas and apply them as you see fit in your relationship.

CoupleCARE is not for severely distressed couples. If you have some serious problems in your relationship, tell your relationship educator. Together you can work out if this program is right for you, or if some other approach would help you improve your relationship.

CoupleCARE is based on 30 years of research and practical experience with couples by our team. The program also builds upon work by other teams around the world. Research consistently shows that doing this program helps build stronger, more positive relationships. We are keep trying to further improve CoupleCARE, and welcome your ideas and suggestions. Please write to us with your comments.

We hope you enjoy and benefit from Couple CARE.

Kim Halford, PhD., FAPsS. Professor of Psychology
Professor of Psychology, University of Queensland

on behalf of the Couple CARE team.

About the Author

Dr. W. Kim Halford is Professor of Clinical Psychology at the University of Queensland in Brisbane, Australia, a position he has held since 2009. From 1995 to 2008 he was Professor of Clinical Psychology at Griffith University, which is also in Brisbane, Australia. He still holds an Honorary Professorship at Griffith University. Before that Kim held a conjoint position as Chief Psychologist at the Royal Brisbane Hospital and Reader in Clinical Psychology at the University of Queensland.

Kim completed a PhD in clinical psychology at La Trobe University in 1979, and is a registered psychologist in Australia, with specialist endorsement as a clinical psychologist.

Kim has been active in research and practice of relationship education and couple therapy for 30 years, and is an internationally known expert on couple relationships. He has held visiting Professorial appointments at the University of Oregon and University of North Carolina in the United States; the University of Manchester in the United Kingdom; the Chinese University of Hong Kong in Hong Kong, China; the University of Zurich in Switzerland; and the University of Tilburg in the Netherlands. Kim has written seven books and over 180 research articles, most of which are on couple relationships. He maintains an active psychological practice working with couples.

What does CoupleCARE involve?

1. A video	The video has 6 units. Each unit is about 12 minutes long. Each unit introduces key ideas and shows key skills.
2. This guidebook	This guidebook also has 6 units. The guidebook helps you apply ideas from the video to your own relationship. You do this with discussion and practical exercises. The discussion and exercises for each unit take about 45 to 50 minutes to complete.
3. Help from a relationship educator.	The relationship educator helps you work through the program. She or he answers any questions you have and helps you develop your relationship skills. You can talk to your educator about any problems you have in practising the skills.

How do we use the video and guidebook?

For each of the 6 units you will need to do the following.

1. Watch the video.

2. Work through the activities in the guidebook for that unit.

3. Discuss the ideas and activities with your relationship educator.

Privacy and using the guidebook

Some activities in this guidebook you do on your own, and some you do together as a couple. The individual activities are labelled 'On your own' and the couple activities are labelled 'As a couple'.

Sometimes you are asked to swap guidebooks with your partner and read what your partner has written. But you will find that most things that you write in your guidebook you can keep private. It is important to respect each other's privacy. Please do not read your partner's guidebook unless your partner invites you to do so.

If you are doing the program at home

Couples often do CoupleCARE at home, usually with telephone or video calls from an educator to help them work through the program. Couples usually get the most out of CoupleCARE when they set aside a particular time each week to work on a unit. (For example, a couple might do it after dinner on a particular night, or might set aside an hour on the weekend.) You should watch a unit of the video together, then do the activities in your guidebooks for that unit. Then talk with your relationship educator at a pre-arranged time. It really helps if you can focus on talking with each other and the educator. Have your guidebooks with you. Switch off the television or any music, ignore your phone, and be mindful about your relationship.

If you are doing the program face-to-face with an educator

CoupleCARE is sometimes completed within face-to-face sessions with a relationship educator. These sessions might be one couple with an educator, or might be run with groups of couples. Talk with your educator about how best to use the program. You will get most from the program if you attend all sessions. If you are completing CoupleCARE with a group of other couples, your educator will discuss the issue of privacy in the first session.

Advice from Couples Who have Done Couple CARE

We asked every couple who have finished the program for advice to give a couple just starting the program. The most common couple advice is the following.

> *'Make the time to do it!!'*

> *'Try to do it when you're feeling fresh, and when you won't be interrupted'.*

> *'Have fun with it, lots of the exercises are fun to try.'*

So, you're ready to start! First step: watch Unit 1 of the video together

Self-Change

Overview

Aims of Unit 1

Part A   To explore your relationship expectations. 'How have my experiences in past relationships influenced my *expectations* of my relationship now?'

Part B   To help you as a couple develop a shared vision for your relationship. 'What sort of relationship do we want to have?'

Part C   To introduce self-change as a way of achieving your relationship vision. 'How can I turn our vision into a reality?

Suggested Unit Activities

As you work through the unit the following activities are suggested.

On your own   Do a written exercise looking at how your past relationship experiences influence your relationship expectations.

As a couple   Discuss the joint strengths and weaknesses of your expectations.

On your own   Write your personal relationship vision.

As a couple   Discuss your relationship visions.

On your own   Develop a self-change plan to enhance your relationship.

Part A: Expectations

Everybody comes into a relationship with ideas about how the relationship should be. These expectations often are not spoken about. As you saw in the video, expectations are often about things like :

- Boundaries (how close versus how independent you should be)

- Power and control (who should make the decisions)

- Investment (how much each of you should put into the relationship)

- Gender roles (what men and women should do in the relationship)

- Extended family (how you relate to close relatives — parents, brothers, sisters, etc.)

Where do relationship expectations come from?

Expectations come from the relationship experiences we have in our lives:

- The people who cared for us when we were young (for most people their parents) have a big influence on us. How they behaved towards each other shapes how we think relationships should be.

- Seeing how other couples behave also gives us ideas. The relationships of family and friends teach us about how relationships should be.

- Most people have relationships with other partners before making a commitment to their current partner. You might have had dating partners, perhaps have lived with someone else, or married someone else, before meeting your current partner.

All the above experiences affect how we think a relationship should be. They guide our ideas on how we want to behave ourselves, and how we want our partner to behave.

Exploring expectations

This activity has 3 parts: (There are spaces over the next few pages where your can write your answers).

1. First, on your own write down your relationship experiences. We ask you to focus on your family of origin (the people with whom you grew up). After that, we ask you to write a little about other relationship experiences.

2. Second, you write down how you think these experiences have influenced your relationship expectations. Then you write down ideas

about which expectations are helpful, and which are unhelpful, to your relationship today.

3. Finally, as a couple you discuss your relationship expectations.

Activity 1.1 My Relationship Experiences

On your own. Reflect on and write down what you saw in your parents' (or other carers') relationship when you were growing up. What was their relationship like? (For example, did they argue a lot? Were they affectionate to each other?) If you grew up in a single parent family, what was your mother or father's relationship like, in general, with other people who were close to them?

What was my parents' or carer's relationship like?

_____

_____

_____

_____

Let's get more specific now. What was your parents or other carers relationship like when it came to the following topics?

Boundaries. (e.g., Did one or both parents/carers believe they should be very close as a couple? Did one or both parents/carers believe that partners should maintain very independent lives?)

_____

_____

_____

_____

Power and control. (Did one parent/carer make most of the decisions? Or was decision-making shared equally? Did one or other parent/carer make most decisions about particular topics, like spending money, or running the household?)

_____

_____

_____

_____

Investment. (e.g., How much time and effort did they invest in their relationship? Did one partner 'give' more?)

_____

_____

_____

_____

Gender roles. (e.g., Did the women in your family tend to do traditional 'female' jobs such as cooking and cleaning? Did the men tend to do 'male' jobs such as gardening and taking out the garbage? Were they able to be flexible?)

_____

_____

_____

_____

Extended Family. (e.g., Did your parents/carers spend lot of time with other relatives such as grandparents, aunts, and uncles? Were people in the extended family an important part of your childhood and adolescence?)

_____

_____

_____

_____

Other relationships. Are there any other relationship experiences that you think are important? It might be other relationships you have seen, or relationships you have been in. Write down the relationship(s), and what you noticed about it. For example, you might have been with a dating partner who drank too much, or was aggressive. Or you might have seen friends who are very loving in how they talk to each other.

_____

_____

_____

_____

Activity 1.2 My Relationship Expectations

On your own. You have looked at the relationship patterns in your family of origin and in other relationships. How do you think these relationship experiences have influenced your *expectations* about how relationships should be? (For example, you might want something you saw in your parents' relationship for your own relationship. Or there might be something you saw, you do not want in your relationship.)

_____

_____

_____

_____

Some of these expectations could have a helpful effect on your relationship. (For example, your mother and father always talked big decisions through and made joint decisions, and you expect to do the same.) Other expectations may be unhelpful. (For example, if your parents argued a lot, you may avoid discussion of difficult issues).

Write down your thoughts on the questions below in the spaces provided.

My expectations that *help* my relationship include:

_____

_____

_____

_____

My expectations that *do not help* my relationship include:

_____

_____

_____

_____

A POINT TO PONDER

Relationship problems can arise if partners hold extreme expectations. For example, if a partner believes that they should control the relationship.

Activity 1.3 Our Relationship Experiences and Expectations

As a couple. Discuss your answers to the following questions.

1. What relationship patterns (from your parent's or other relationship) do you want in your own relationship? Which patterns would you like to avoid?

2. How do you think your relationship with each of your parents has influenced your emotional health as an adult?

As a couple. Discuss your answers to the exercise above 'My expectations that help …' and 'My expectations that don't help …'.

Write down what you see as your joint **strengths and areas to work on** in terms of relationship expectations.

As a couple we think our joint strengths are:

_____

_____

_____

_____

As a couple we think areas we need to work upon are:

_____

_____

_____

_____

A POINT TO PONDER

Relationship problems can arise if partners have very different expectations. Talking about expectations is one way to help agree on what you want. It is common for a couple to find that there are some differences in their expectations. If such differences do arise, remember that it is an accepted part of exploring issues together. Hang in there, the skills you will learn throughout the program will help you talk through these differences.

Part B: Developing a Relationship Vision

What does a great relationship look like?

So far in this unit you have been asked to think about things that have influenced your ideas about relationships. Having thought about this, we suggest you develop a relationship vision. A relationship vision is:

- A 'word picture' of how you want your relationship to be.

- Something only you can define. Great relationships are not all the same.

- How you would really like to be as a couple.

- Specific. How your idea show themselves in every day actions.

Activity 1.4 Describing A Great Relationship

To get started, **as a couple,** think of another couple you know who have been together at least 5 years and who are happy.

Write down their first names.

_____

What do you like about how they act as a couple?

_____

_____

_____

_____

Defining your relationship vision

Now, remember back to the couple looking at photos in the video. They were thinking about all the things they had done together. Imagine you are 20 or 30 years into the future looking back on your relationship. How would you like your relationship to be through those years? How will you act toward each other? What things will you want to have done as a couple?

Activity 1.5 My Ideas on a Relationship Vision

On your own. Write down your ideas for your own relationship vision.

_____

_____

_____

_____

_____

_____

_____

_____

_____

Next, **as a couple** compare your vision with your partner's vision. Note down the similarities in your visions. It is likely there will be some differences as well. Just note down the differences and try to understand your partner's point of view.

Write down you *Similarities*

_____

_____

_____

Write down your *Differences*

_____

_____

_____

_____

Did you notice some things in your partner's vision that you liked that were not in your vision? Note them below.

Things I liked in my partner's vision but I had not thought of myself:

_____

_____

_____

_____

A POINT TO PONDER

A relationship vision is not fixed. It develops and changes over time. Total agreement between the two of you on your relationship visions is not needed, just a commitment to keep talking and thinking.

So, you've thought about how you would like your relationship to be. How can you best turn it into a reality? Part 3 of this unit introduces **self-change** as a great tool for making your vision come alive now and grow in the future.

Part C: Self-Change

What is self-change?

Self-change is planning and making changes to your own behaviour in order to enhance your relationship. For example, if 'being loving' is part of your relationship vision, what specific things can you do, on a day-to-day basis, that will keep your relationship loving?

Self-change has 4 steps:

1. DESCRIBE the issue in clear and specific terms.

2. FOCUS on your own behaviour.

3. SET A GOAL — define what you will do positively.

4. EVALUATE — how did it go?

Describe. This is thinking about how your relationship is going, choosing one thing you would like to improve, and then describing it clearly. Focus on key areas that really make a difference to relationships. (The 6 units of Couple CARE reflect the areas known to be most important in relationships).

Focus on your own behaviour. You have most influence over your own actions, so think about what *you* currently do. Examine the pluses and minuses of how *you* behave to help work out what you can do differently. Focusing on your own behaviour does not mean you ignore what your partner does. However, you should start with what *you* do. For example, if your partner is doing something that you would like to change, reflect on *how* you have talked to your partner about that issue.

Set a Goal. Think about what you want in the relationship. Define exactly what *you* will do to achieve your relationship goal. Set a time limit on when to take your action.

Evaluate. Did you do what you said you would do? What effect did it have on your relationship? Then decide if you need to take further action. For example, if what you did was helpful, how can you continue to do it? Should you do it a little differently next time?

It is harder to change someone else's behaviour. You have much more control over your own.

An example of self-change

Let's look back at the way the man in the video tried to work towards self-change to improve his relationship. What did he do, and how can you apply these ideas?

1. Describe	2. Focus
He thought about wanting to have quality time with his partner. He thought about what was happening in the relationship regarding this issue. He described what happened clearly and positively (avoiding blame and negativity). *You can use the same idea and think about something you want to work on in your relationship.*	He thought about what he was currently doing. He weighed up the pluses and minuses of his attempt to go out with his partner. *You can reflect on what you do at the moment, and the pluses and minuses of what you do.*
3. Set a Goal	**4. Evaluate**
He chose a goal to try to make things better. His goal was clear and specific. He thought about exactly what he wanted to say. *When you set goals you need to define what you want to do clearly and specifically. You need to ask yourself:* • *What exactly will I do?* • *When will I do it?* • *Where will I do it?*	Afterwards he thought about how it went. He reflected on what he did, and what effect it had on his partner and his relationship. *After you try self-change, you might like to ask yourself these questions:* • *Did I do what I meant to?* • *What were the effects (positive and negative) of what you did?* • *If it went well, how will I continue the changes made?* • *If it did not work out, how can I adjust my plan and try again?*

Let's look closely at what is meant by some of the terms we have used in describing how to do self-change well.

In Step 1 you are asked to define the issue *clearly* and *positively*. In Step 3 you are asked to set a goal. The goal needs to be *specific*, *realistic*, and *time-limited*. The table below defines what we mean by these words, and gives examples.

Definition	Poor Example	Good Example
Clear: Be specific and concrete about what happens and when.	We sometimes fight.	After work on busy days, I tend to argue about little things such as whose turn it is to cook.
	We never have time to see each other.	On weekends we each have lots of things we do. We have not gone out as a couple, just the two of us, for 7 weeks. I want to go out together more than that.
Positive: Think about what you *do* want, not what you *don't* want in the relationship. Avoid blaming the other person for things you do not like.	I hate the way we never spend any time together.	I would like to spend more time with my partner.
Specific: Be precise rather than vague about your action plan. Try to focus on behaviours that can be seen.	I want to feel closer my partner.	I would like discuss my work and hobbies, which are important to me, with my partner.
Realistic: Select actions you are likely to be able to do.	I will never get angry again.	I will try to be calm, to listen to her and speak quietly, when we next talk about this issue.
	I will shower my partner with presents	Tomorrow I will stop at the shops on the way home from work and buy my partner something I know she'll like — a mango.
Time-limited: Define when you will do your actions.	From now on I will cuddle my partner more	This week, I will cuddle my partner for a few minutes each morning before I get out of bed.

Activity 1.6 Using Self-Change

Okay, now let's tackle an issue to enhance your own relationship.

On your own. Pick one area in your relationship vision that you would like to improve. Choose an area that is important to you. Follow the four steps in the box on page 15 opposite. If this exercise seems difficult at first, don't worry, as your telephone educator will review the self-change steps with you.

1. Describe

Choose an issue you'd like to work on that involves changing something about your behaviour. Describe this aspect clearly and positively (write in the spaces provided).

_____

_____

_____

2. Focus

What do I currently do?

_____

_____

What are the **pluses** of my current behaviour?

_____

_____

What are the **minuses** of my current behaviour?

_____

_____

3. Set a Goal

Define exactly what I want to do. Where and when will I do it?

_____

_____

_____

What might get in the way? How will I make sure it happens?

_____

_____

4. Evaluate (Afterwards)

What did I actually do?

_____

_____

What **positives** resulted?

_____

_____

What **negatives** resulted?

_____

_____

What do I do from here?

_____

_____

A Few Ideas on the Different Ways People Learn

We each have different ways we prefer to learn. Some of us prefer to be told things, and have those ideas set out clearly. Some of us prefer to discover things for ourselves, and dislike being told things. As you reflect on the first unit you might like to think about the way you learn.

In CoupleCARE we try to use a mix of giving information and helping people to discover things through doing the activities. You might like to try learning in ways you might not have done in the past. If you like to be told things, try being open to discovery through the activities provided in the program. If you're used to working things out for yourself, try to be open to learning through a more structured approach.

A POINT TO PONDER

Each of us has our own particular way of learning. It's important to uncover our preferred learning style because we often learn faster that way. But it also is important to be open to new ways of learning.

Any questions?

Do you have any questions, worries, or ideas that occur to you about Unit 1? You can note them down here. Please feel free to raise them with your educator.

_____

_____

_____

_____

Congratulations!

You have worked through Unit 1. The remaining units in the workbook all follow a similar pattern. There is a mixture of individual and couple activities to do after you have watched the video. There is a self-change plan at the end for you to put into action what you have been thinking and talking about.

Communication

Overview

Aims of Unit 2

Part A   To help you understand the key elements of good communication. 'How do I avoid the problem of "But I didn't mean that!" or "I just don't understand you."'

Part B   To look at how you communicate now, develop ideas about what you do well, and identify areas you might want to improve. 'What I am like as a listener? Do I get my message across as clearly as I can?'

Part C   To explore self-disclosure (direct statement of feelings) and emotional bidding (subtle, indirect communication) in your relationship.

Part D   To help you improve your communication by focusing on what you can do. 'How can I express myself so my partner understands me? How do I listen so my partner feels understood?'

Suggested Unit Activities

As you work through the unit the following activities will be suggested.

On your own   Check your memory of the intent-impact model of communication shown in the video.

As a couple   Talk for about 5 minutes being a listener, and talk for 5 minutes as a speaker. You self-evaluate your communication in those discussions.

As a couple   Talk about self-disclosure, and emotional bids, in your relationship.

On your own   Write a self-change plan to enhance your communication.

Reflecting on Unit 1...

Think about what you did in Unit 1 — Self-Change. Write down any ideas that you liked. How have you used these ideas since you did Unit 1 (even if only in a small way)?

Ideas I liked:

_____

_____

_____

How I have used the ideas:

_____

_____

_____

How did you go carrying out your self-change plan from Unit 1?

_____

_____

_____

_____

Circle the number that best describes how far you went in doing your self-change plan.

very poor/					OK, did try				excellent	
did not do anything									did it all	
0	1	2	3	4	5	6	7	8	9	10

Part A: What *is* good communication?

Communicating well brings a sense of connection with your partner. It helps you to know your partner, and for her or him to know you. Have you had special moments with your partner when you have communicated well? At such times you probably felt understood at a deep level. You also probably felt you understood your partner. These times allow your relationship to grow. You feel close to your partner.

On the other hand, have you ever had times when the communication was poor? You may have felt unable to put your ideas and feelings into words, or that the words kept coming out wrong. Or you thought your partner meant one thing, but they really meant something quite different.

So what do we actually *do* when we're communicating well?

Ten Key Communication Skills

There are ten very important skills when it comes to communicating well. These can be divided into four speaker skills and six listener skills.

Speaker Skills

1. **Describe specifics:** provide clear and concrete descriptions of behaviours or situations.

2. **Be assertive:** clearly express your thoughts and feelings about the positive aspects of a situation or your partner's behaviour, even if things seem mostly negative.

3. **Sensitively express negatives:** without being aggressive or attacking, say directly what you dislike or want to change.

4. **Self-disclose feelings:** share your thoughts and feelings with your partner even if it feels difficult.

Listener skills

5. **Attend:** focus your attention on your partner when they are speaking. This includes having eye contact, facing your partner, and removing distractions (e.g., put down the newspaper, switch off your phone).

6. **Encourage:** this involves saying things like 'Oh.', 'Go on.' or 'I see.' so your partner knows you're interested in what he/she is saying.

7. **Summarise content:** state back to your partner **in your own words** the **key points** of what he/she has just said.

8. **Summarise feeling:** summarise in words the emotion your partner is expressing. Often their emotion will not be said in words, but will be reflected in how they say things, and how they look.

9. **Ask questions:** ask open-ended questions that encourage your partner to open up their ideas.

10. **Hear your partner out:** Let your partner finish speaking, do not interrupt, avoid immediately disagreeing, or defending yourself. Put your own opinion on hold until later.

On the page opposite is a summarised list of these ten skills that you might like to take a copy of and stick on the frdige as a reminder.

10 Key Communication Skills

Speaking

1. Describe specifics
2. Be assertive
3. Sensitively express negatives
4. Self-disclose feelings

Listening

5. Attend
6. Encourage
7. Summarise content
8. Summarise feelings
9. Ask questions
10. Hear your partner out

Part B: How am I communicating now?

Activity 2.1 Assessing Your Communication in a Discussion

As a couple, we want you to develop your communication. This exercise involves you and your partner having a planned discussion together. The aim is for you each to see how you are communicating now.

For this exercise you will need:

• a watch or smart phone, and

• a quiet time and place

Here's what to do: Talk with your partner about an activity he or she really enjoys, or a social issue he or she feels strongly about. Have them choose an activity or issue you do not know much about. Your task is to try to understand their interest in this activity or issue. So don't talk about **your** ideas or interests, or try to persuade your partner to change. Simply try to respect and understand their point of view. Stop after two to three minutes. Then swap roles so that you and your partner chat about an issue or activity that **you** really enjoy. Again, talk for two to three minutes.

When you have everything you need and you are ready to start, follow the steps below.

First, **on your own,** each of you choose a topic. (Remember, the topic you each choose should be something you enjoy, are interested in or feel strongly about.).

Then, think about how you would like to communicate with your partner about their topic and write down your personal goals for the discussion in the *My Communication Goals* box below. Look at the *Ten Key Communication Skills* list on page 21 when setting your goals. Try to choose just one or two communication goals.

My Communication Goals

In my discussion with my partner I have the following goal/s for my communication (be as specific as possible):

_____

_____

_____

As a couple, appoint one partner to act as timekeeper. Read out to each other your goal statements for the conversation. Then decide who is going to be first to talk about their chosen topic. Hold the discussion. After two to three minutes, swap over

On your own, evaluate you own communication using the *Communication Self-Evaluation Form* over the page on page 24. Then, complete your points of strengths and the things you need to improve on. Make sure you complete this task before moving on to the giving and receiving feedback task below.

Giving and Receiving Feedback

What is feedback? Feedback is discussing with our partner our ideas about their strengths and also our suggestions for change in their behaviour.

Giving feedback works best when:

• The feedback starts with positive comments about strengths.

• Suggestions for change are offered gently, as ideas to consider, not as criticisms or commands.

• You ask for reactions to the feedback (e.g., What do you think of that suggestion?)

Receiving feedback works best when:

• You listen to all the feedback and do not interrupt.

• You use your listener skills to really understand the feedback.

• You avoid becoming defensive.

Activity 2.2 An Exercise on Feedback

In this exercise you do two things.

On your own, think back to the discussions you just had with your partner, write down two *positives* about how your partner communicated with you and one *suggestion for change* in the space below.

1st Positive (be specific)

_____

_____

Communication Self-Evaluation Form

Date:_____

On your own, place a tick to describe how **you** think you went during the discussion using this key. (Don't feel that you have to have used all the 10 skills):

- 0   No use of this skill
- 1   Some use of this skill
- 2   OK, but could be better
- 3   Good use of this skill
- N/A   Skill not applicable

SKILL	0	1	2	3	N/A
Speaker Skills					
Described specifics	☐	☐	☐	☐	☐
Assertive	☐	☐	☐	☐	☐
Sensitively expressed negatives	☐	☐	☐	☐	☐
Self-disclosed feelings	☐	☐	☐	☐	☐
Listener Skills					
Attended	☐	☐	☐	☐	☐
Encouraged	☐	☐	☐	☐	☐
Summarised content	☐	☐	☐	☐	☐
Summarised feelings	☐	☐	☐	☐	☐
Asked question	☐	☐	☐	☐	☐
Heard my partner out	☐	☐	☐	☐	☐

My strengths in the communication:

_____

_____

_____

Things I need to work on in communication:

_____

_____

_____

2nd positive

_____

_____

A suggestion for change:

_____

_____

A POINT TO PONDER

Do the skills we described capture what you think is good communication? What else might be important?

Next, **as a couple**, give each other the feedback you have just recorded. Note down, and be prepared to discuss with your relationship educator, the feedback you received from your partner.

Part C: Self-Disclosure and Emotional Bids

The video for this unit introduced the ideas of *self-disclosure* and *emotional bids*. Self-disclosures are direct statements of feelings. Self-disclosure is often about very personal feelings, and the person self-disclosing often feels vulnerable. For example, telling your partner how much you love them. Emotional bids are subtle, indirect ways of asking for intimacy from your partner. For example, you commenting to your partner that the room is cold could be an emotional bid for a cuddle, for attention from your partner.

Self-disclosures help partners to understand each other at a deep level. They often build intimacy and closeness. Emotional bids also serve a purpose in relationships. As emotional bids are indirect, they reduce the chance of obvious rejection. The partner can fail to respond to the emotional bid without being overtly rejecting. For example, your partner might respond to your comment that the room is cold by turning on a heater, or by commenting that they do not feel cold.

Most couples use self-disclosure and emotional bids at times in their relationships.

Activity 2.3 Self-disclosure and Emotional Bids in Your Relationship

On your own, write down an example of a self-disclosure and an emotional bid you have made toward your partner.

An example of a self-disclosure I have made in my relationship:

_____

_____

An example of an emotional bid I have made in my relationship.

_____

_____

As a couple, discuss the pluses of the use of self-disclosure and emotional bids in your relationship. Also discuss the minuses of self-disclosure and emotional bids. Then write down some of things you came up with.

The pluses of self-disclosure:

_____

The minuses of self-disclosure:

_____

_____

_____

The pluses of emotional bids:

_____

_____

_____

The minuses of emotional bids:

_____

_____

_____

Part D: Improving my communication

Now you have a framework for understanding communication. You also have ideas of what your communication is like, both your strengths and areas to work on. The next step is to use *self-change* to improve your communication.

Remember — it's much *harder* to change someone else's behaviour. You have much more control over your *own*. Keeping this in mind, let's use the four steps of self-change to enhance your own communication.

Self-Change Plan for Communication

1. Describe	2. Focus
Choose an aspect of your communication you want to improve. Describe this aspect clearly and positively (write in the spaces provided). _____ _____ _____ _____	What do I currently do? _____ _____ What are the **pluses** of my current behaviour? _____ _____ What are the **minuses** of my current behaviour? _____ _____
3. Set a Goal	**4. Evaluate (Afterwards)**
Define exactly what I want to do. Where and when will I do it? _____ _____ _____ What might get in the way? How will I make sure it happens? _____ _____ _____	What did I actually do? _____ _____ What **positives** resulted? _____ _____ What **negatives** resulted? _____ _____ What do I do from here? _____ _____

I was wondering ...

Note down any questions, concerns, worries, thoughts, or ideas you have about Unit 2. Your relationship educator is available to discuss issues or answer questions.

_____

_____

_____

_____

_____

Intimacy and Caring

Overview

Aims of Unit 3

Part A   To explore how you show caring now, and how you can express caring more fully. 'What can I do that shows I really care?'

Part B   To review the balance of individual and couple interests and activities in your life. 'How do we balance being individuals and being a couple?'

Part C   To reflect on how you celebrate your relationship. 'What do we do to remind ourselves how important our relationship is to us?'

Suggested Unit Activities

As you work through this unit the following activities will be suggested.

On your own   Review how you currently express caring within your relationship, and think about other ways to express that caring.

As a couple   Discuss ideas you have for new ways to show caring to each other.

On your own   Review how you currently spend your time as an individual and as a couple, and to what extent you would like to change that mix.

As a couple   Review how you currently celebrate your relationship.

On your own   Do a self-change plan for enhancing caring and intimacy.

Reflecting on Unit 2...

Think about what you did Unit 2 — Communication. Write down any ideas that you liked. How have you used these ideas since you did the unit (even if only in a small way)?

Ideas I liked:

_____

_____

_____

How I have used the ideas:

_____

_____

_____

How did you go carrying out your self-change plan from Unit 1?

_____

_____

_____

_____

Circle the number that best describes how far you went in doing your self-change plan.

very poor/ did not do anything					OK, did try				excellent did it all	
0	1	2	3	4	5	6	7	8	9	10

Part A: Showing Caring

Caring is doing small acts that express your positive feelings toward your partner. It is a concrete way of showing that you love your partner, you like them as a person, and you value them as a friend.

A POINT TO PONDER

When couples first get together they tend to do lots of caring things for each other. However, after a while these acts of caring can drop off. Happy couples tend to keep showing caring. Are you, as a couple, showing caring as much as did when you first started seeing each other?

Activity 3.1 How do I usually show I care?

On your own, write down below what have you done to show your partner you care.

Today:

_____

_____

Yesterday:

_____

_____

What *new* caring things have you done in the past 3 months? (That is, things you had not done before?

_____

_____

_____

_____

A POINT TO PONDER

Most people find doing new things to show you care is important. What new things could you do to show caring? What do your friends do to show they care about their partner?

Activity 3.2 Giving and Receiving Feedback on Caring

On the opposite page (page 35) is a form to guide you in giving and receiving feedback on showing caring in your relationship.

On your own, in the top half of the box in column 1A make a list of caring behaviours your partner does for you. Pick those caring acts that you really like. In column 2A rate how much you like those behaviours as a way of showing caring of you from 1 = *a little positive* to 10 = *extremely positive.*

In the bottom half of the box in column 1B write down some possible *new* caring behaviours you could do for your partner. You might include things you used to do, but have not done for a while. You also might include things you have never done.

Next, **as a couple** swap your guidebooks. Discuss your lists with each other. Ask your partner to rate from 1 = *a little positive* to 10 = *extremely positive* how positive they feel about each caring behaviour listed in column 1B of the bottom box. Ask your partner to write down their rating in column 2B of the bottom box.

Now it is time to start thinking about a *self-change plan* for caring. Have a look through the Ideas for Caring Behaviours listed on pages 36 and 37. Tick three or four items in the list you might do soon to show caring for your partner. Add any ideas from Columns 1A and 1B of the previous exercise that are not in the list. You might want to use these ideas to develop a change plan for caring for your partner (see page 48).

Caring Behaviours Checklist

1A Caring things my partner does for me.	2A Self-rating of how positive (from 1 to 10)

1B Possible new caring behaviours I could do for my partner	2B Partner rating of how positive (from 1 to 10)

Ideas for Caring Behaviours

Getting a household repair done	Balancing the chequebook
Preparing an entire meal	Paying a bill
Helping with the dinner	Doing some needed gardening
Taking care of the car	Doing the dishes
Doing some shopping for things we need	Cleaning or straightening up a bit
Doing the laundry	Mending my partner's clothes
Doing an errand	Mowing the lawn
Taking out the garbage	Setting the alarm clock
Feeding or taking care of the pets	Having an enjoyable conversation
Telling my partner something confidential	Making some extra money
Starting a conversation with my partner	Summarising my partner's point of view
Asking my partner how he/she feels so she/he knows I am listening	Doing something my partner asked
Forgiving my partner for something	Helping to dress the children
Giving my partner a nice greeting	Asking for my partner's opinion
when we meet after being apart	Smiling at my partner or laughing with him/her
Giving my partner a massage or rub down	Initiating sex
Talking to my partner when he/she asks for some attention	Hire a video
Being nice to my partner's friends	Trying to cheer my partner up
Touching my partner affectionately	Paying my partner a compliment
Being nice to my partner even though he/she was mean	Looking nice (dress, shaving, etc)
Hugging or kissing my partner	Praising my partner

Making his/her favourite food	Responding to sexual advances
Cuddling	Bringing my partner a present
Doing something sexual he/she really likes	Showing that sex was enjoyable
Talking together about finances to help us stick to the budget	Shopping for something together
Talking about his/her friends or relatives	Going out to dinner, movie or a tavern
Talking together about making a purchase	Playing sports together
Spending time together having fun	Playing games together
Planning or helping with a social event	Suggesting something fun for us to do
Doing something together in the evening	

Caring Behaviours my Partner suggested that I would be keen to do:

_____

_____

_____

_____

Part B: Balancing Time Use

In a healthy relationship, the couple balances the time they spend doing things individually, the time they spend doing things together as a couple, and the time they share as a couple with other people. There is no one correct balance. Each couple needs to find the balance that suits them.

We each need *individual interests* to develop our own unique selves. No two people have the same interests. Maintaining individual interests and hobbies brings new ideas and experiences into your relationship.

Time *together* with just the two of you heightens your sense of closeness. It allows you to have fun together that is just between to the two of you. It provides special time to communicate privately as a couple.

Shared activities *with others*, such as family and friends, bring fun and variety into your lives. It helps builds a network of people outside your relationship who can be there for you.

If the balance of individual, couple and shared activities does not feel right, problems can develop.

- Couples who have too little individual time often say they feel a loss of sense of self. They may have little interesting to say to each other, because the partner is almost always present.

- Couples who have very little couple time often feel a loss of intimacy. They may find it hard to get the chance to talk to each other about issues that are concerning them.

- Couples with few joint activities shared with others may feel cut off as a couple from friends and extended family.

Activity 3.3 What is my current mix of activities?

On your own. Fill in the following boxes on *regular* activities you do. Regular means you do this at least every 2 to 3 months.

My Current Regular Activities

Individual activities without your partner:

_____

_____

_____

_____

_____

Couple Activities (just the two of you):

_____

_____

_____

_____

_____

Shared activities with your partner and others.

_____

_____

_____

_____

_____

What did you discover from doing the exercise on the previous page? Which boxes did you fill up the most? Which ones were the emptiest?

Now, **on your own,** tick the boxes below that apply to you.

☐ I would like more *independent* activities.

☐ I would like fewer *independent* activities.

☐ I would like some new *independent* activities.

☐ I am happy with my *independent* activities as they are, no changes are needed.

☐ I would like more *couple* activities with my partner.

☐ I would like fewer *couple* activities with my partner.

☐ I would like some new *couple* activities with my partner.

☐ I am happy with our *couple* activities, no changes are needed.

☐ I would like more *shared* activities with my partner and others.

☐ I would like fewer *shared* activities with my partner and others.

☐ I would like some new *shared* activities with my partner and others.

☐ I am happy with my *shared* activities, no changes are needed.

How do you feel about your current mix of activities?

As a couple discuss your answers to the 'My Current Regular Activities' exercise. How similar were you and your partner's responses?

Now consult the 'Guidelines for Activity Discussion' below to consider what you want to do next.

Guidelines for discussion about your balance of activities

If you both are happy with your balance of activities

That is great. But remember, you need to keep an eye on your balance of activities. Lots of things can change the balance. For example, changes at work, in extended family, having a baby, or just the need for something new, can shift the balance.

If you both want similar changes in your balance of activities

You can plan as a couple to make some changes.

- If you would both like to bring more (or more varied) couple activities into your life, you may like to make a list of interests you both share. See the list *Ideas for Couple Activities* on page 42.

- If you would like to bring more individual activities into your life, you may like to make a list of your personal interests (perhaps ones you haven't followed up for a while). See the *Ideas for Individual Activities* on page 45.

- If you would like to bring about more shared activities with others, you may like to make a list of mutual friends and family and activities you may like to do with them.

If you seem to want a somewhat different balance from each other

A common experience for couples occurs when one partner wants more time in independent activities and the other partner wants more time in couple activities. This problem can sometimes feel difficult to resolve. The more each partner pushes to have what they want, the more the other pushes for the opposite. If this issue seems familiar to you, here are some ideas:

1. Reflect on your expectations about boundaries from your family of origin (see Unit 1, page 3). How have these influenced your expectations for your relationship? How do you think your partner's family-of-origin experiences have affected your partner's expectations about your relationship?

2. Self-change can help. Remember that it's hard to change your partner's behaviour; it's easier to change your own. As you change yourself (e.g., become more flexible and open to your partner's wishes, or try a different way of telling your partner how you feel) you may find the problem loses its power.

3. Look for a creative solution. For example, perhaps you can both have what you want by both planning more shared activities *and* more

individual activities. Or, if you are the one desiring more couple activities, adding some *different* couple activities that your partner enjoys a lot may change his/her attitude to shared time. Also, agreeing to work on solo projects more, but doing it when your partner is there, can enhance feelings of togetherness and you still get your own thing done.

4. In next week's unit we talk about *managing differences*. You may find more ideas there.

You might want to do a self-change plan for your balance of activities. You can use information from your couple discussion and ideas from the folowing lists to help you come up with a plan.

Ideas for Couple Activities

Going bicycle riding before Sunday breakfast	Doing jobs together — wasting an hour or two driving around, going into different shops to get things
Visiting friends	Camping
Having a shower or bath together	Playing pool
Visiting a museum or art gallery together	Daydreaming about a fantastic holiday you know you can't afford
Playing scrabble together	Starting an aquarium
Renting a rowboat or canoe for the afternoon	Playing tennis
Going to a sporting event (basketball, football, cricket)	Writing letters to friends
Going on a picnic	Jogging
Making wine together	Playing charades
Doing relaxation exercises or meditating together	Reading a play aloud
Reading the weekend papers together	Gardening together
Taking dancing lessons	Doing the bills together
Playing frisbee	Going to a bar and talking
Going to a festival/ markets	Treating yourselves to a big breakfast of pancakes, eggs, bacon, orange juice, toast
Making a collage	Going to a concert
Going sailing	Going to the beach

Playing music together (guitar, piano, etc)

Visiting a National Park with a waterfall

Going to see a band

Playing golf (or miniature golf) together

Going to the race track

Watching TV together

Playing cards

Stargazing: lying on your back and
learning to recognise all the
constellations and bright stars

Working for a political candidate

Painting the house

Calling up an old mutual friend
on the phone long-distance

Climbing a mountain

Turning down the sound on the TV
and making up funny scripts

Planning a family reunion

Gossiping

Going roller-blading

Riding bikes together

Going for a drive

Visiting a brand new interesting place

Eating pizza (at home or at a restaurant)

Washing the car

Inviting someone new over for dinner
or drinks

Going to church

Going to a movie together

Baking bread together

Going skating

Going window shopping together

Buying fish and chips

Just sitting around with the lights low
and talking

Going to the botanical gardens

Buying a new CD together

Cooking an exciting meal together

Going second-hand shopping

Making home-made pizzas and throwing
lots of stuff on them

Browsing in a bookstore together

Backpacking

Meeting for lunch or coffee during the day

Having a BBQ in the park together

Flying a kite

Doing exercises (yoga, dance, aerobics)

Joining a new group or club together

Looking at slides, photos or home movies
for a day

Going horseback riding

Watching late movies on TV and
cuddling during the commercials

Going out to eat

Playing in the rain or leaves

Reading in bed together

Working on crafts together, (tie-dying,
pottery, candle-making etc)

Listening to music	Fishing
Talking about day-to-day happenings	Making love
Exploring new places, places you'd never usually go (junkyard, new bars, new areas of town)	Watercolouring or fingerpainting
Hanging out in a new coffee shop talking and trying out new coffees	Making or planning home improvements
Going swimming in the nude	Getting up to see the sunrise
Playing with pets	Going to the opera or ballet
Spending a romantic evening alone (dinner, candlelight, music)	Eating breakfast out
Going to a play	Reading poetry out loud
Going to an auction	Reading science fiction or mysteries out loud in bed at night
Taking a picnic lunch to a nearby park and going hiking together or with friends	Going to a party
Going to the library; browsing through the books and records together	Inviting old friends over for Sunday lunch
Going swimming	Going dancing (ballroom, folkdancing, square dancing)
Arranging and taking pictures	Cooking something you've never cooked before
Going on a shopping spree	Buying new home decorations
Giving a party	Going for a walk in the bush or forest
Eating and talking together	Doing a jigsaw or crossword puzzle together
Sunbaking	Looking around in secondhand or antique shops
Going to a motel for the night	

Ideas for Individual Activities

Creative Activities

Doing art work

Doing pottery, ceramics

Knitting, needlework, or sewing

Taking a course in a creative skill (e.g. art, photography, cooking, or pottery)

Cooking something special or new

Redecorating

Restoring furniture or antiques

Doing woodwork or carpentry

Repairing things

Working with machines, engines, or electrical equipment

Photography

Writing

Thinking up or arranging songs or music

Singing or dancing

Playing a musical instrument

Learning to play a musical instrument

Acting or taking acting lessons

Participating in creative interests

Reading books, articles, magazines related to your creative interests

Entertainment Activities

Watching TV

Listening to the radio

Listening to music

Going to a play or drama

Seeing a film

Going to concerts, opera, ballet

Going to an art gallery, exhibition, or museum

Going to see a band

Going to a sports event

Going to the races (car, boat or horse)

Educational Activities

Reading books, plays or poems which which interest you

Reading academic literature on a subject which interests you

Going to lecture courses or other classes

Learning a foreign language

Going to the library

Learning to do something new (e.g. acquiring a new skill)

Physical Activities

Playing tennis or squash

Playing golf

Going boating or sailing

Going fishing

Going hiking, mountain climbing, or camping

Going swimming, diving, or surfing

Playing basketball or netball	Going bowling, skating, or playing pool
Going jogging, running or bicycle riding	Going horseback riding
Going to the gym or doing weight-lifting	Driving a 4WD, sports car, or motorcycle for the sheer fun of it
Other Activities	
Having an active involvement in politics, community, or social action groups	Being involved in religious or church activities
Speaking a foreign language	Playing chess or draughts
Buying something for yourself	
Collecting things (e.g., stamps, coins, or wine)	Gathering natural objects (flowers, rocks, or driftwood)
Gardening	Visiting interesting outdoor places (e.g., zoo, parks, riverside, or harbour)
Caring for or being with animals or pets	Being in the country or mountains
Having or planning a holiday (on your own)	Having massages or back rubs
Going to a sauna or doing health-related activities	Doing yoga or meditation

Part C: Celebrate Your Relationship

As discussed in the video, celebrating your relationship is another important way you can focus on the positives in your relationship. Most couples develop rituals that focus them on their relationship. It might be a special dinner on their anniversary, a birthday together, or holiday time. Each couple is different and it is not important how you celebrate your relationship. But, it is important that you do celebrate.

> 'It's our wedding anniversary next week. Every year for the last 15 years we have gone to dinner, just the two of us. Except in 2010, when I was in labour with Jeffrey. Last year we went on to a coffee place. Mike smuggled in a photo album which had some of our wedding shots, and when the kids were babies. Looking over that together was the most romantic experience of my life.'

> 'This year I've got something to surprise Mike. I got a photo from his mum of us going out way back before we were married. He had this dreadful beard and a large tattoo, my dad hated him. He'll die when he sees the beard.'

> 'For me Friday nights are special. It's the end of the week. Even if you're beat, you've got the weekend to enjoy stuff. Most weeks we sit on our front porch and have a drink. Often we plan what we're going to do in the next week or two, or bitch about work, or just catch up on stuff. I love it.'

Activity 3.4 Reviewing and Developing Celebration Rituals

On your own write down any ways that you celebrate your relationship with your partner. Celebrations can take many forms: a drink together, a romantic weekend, looking at photos, or having a special meal.

Some ways we celebrate our relationship are:

_____

_____

_____

As a couple, talk about how you do, and how you want to, celebrate your relationship. Write down two rituals you want to have.

Celebration 1. When, where and how:

_____

_____

Celebration 2. When, where and how:

_____

_____

Activity 3.5 Self-Change Plan

On your own reflect on the ideas that have been covered in this unit. Pick one are of your relationship related to intimacy and caring that you would like to work on. Write a self-change plan in the space provided on the next page.

Self-Change Plan for Intimacy and Caring

1. Describe	2. Focus
Choose an issue about intimacy and caring you'd like to work on that involves changing something about your behaviour. Describe this aspect clearly and positively (write in the spaces provided). _____ _____ _____ _____	What do I currently do? _____ _____ What are the **pluses** of my current behaviour? _____ _____ What are the **minuses** of my current behaviour? _____ _____
3. Set a Goal	**4. Evaluate (Afterwards)**
Define exactly what I want to do. Where and when will I do it? _____ _____ _____ What might get in the way? How will I make sure it happens? _____ _____ _____	What did I actually do? _____ _____ What **positives** resulted? _____ _____ What **negatives** resulted? _____ _____ What do I do from here? _____ _____

I was wondering ...

Note down any questions, concerns, worries, thoughts, or ideas you have about Unit 3. Your relationship educator is available to discuss issues or answer questions.

_____

_____

_____

_____

_____

Congratulations!

You are now half way through the Couple CARE program. We hope you are enjoying the activities. Please feel free to discuss your reactions to the program (positive or negative) with your educator.

Managing Differences

Overview

Aims of Unit 4

Part A   To review how you manage differences now. 'Which areas do we have disagreements about? What patterns do we show when we have conflict?'

Part B   To assess and improve your conflict management.

Part C   To review how you recover after conflict with your partner, and whether that can be improved.

Suggested Unit Activities

As you work through this unit the following activities will be suggested.

On your own   Identify which areas you and your partner disagree about.

As a couple   Identify the patterns in how you manage conflict between you.

As a couple   Set some 'ground rules' for when you have conflict

As a couple   Discuss a difficult issue, assess how you manage the conflict, and give each other some feedback.

As a couple   Look at how you two recover after an argument and consider some ideas for improving recovery.

A POINT TO PONDER

Often we are attracted to someone because they are different from us. Sometimes these differences also have aspects that we find difficult to deal with. For example, the outgoing partner who brings us out of ourselves can also lead us to feel embarrassed in some social situations. Do you recognise any differences like this in your relationship?

Reflecting on Unit 3...

Think about what you did in Unit 3 — Intimacy and Caring. Write down any ideas that you liked. How have you used these ideas since doing Unit 3 (even if only in a small way)?

Ideas I liked:

_____

_____

_____

How I have used the ideas:

_____

_____

_____

How did you go carrying out your self-change plan from Unit 1?

_____

_____

_____

_____

Circle the number that best describes how far you went in doing your self-change plan.

very poor/ did not do anything					OK, did try				excellent did it all	
0	1	2	3	4	5	6	7	8	9	10

Part A: How do we currently manage our differences?

Activity 4.1 In what areas do my partner and I have differences?

Most couples have disagreements. **On your own**, tick the answer that best describes how often you disagree about each area listed. Write in the last two rows any other topics about which you disagree.

	Always Agree	Almost Always Agree	Occasionally Disagree	Frequently Disagree	Almost Always Disagree	Always Disagree
Handling family finances	☐	☐	☐	☐	☐	☐
Matters of recreation	☐	☐	☐	☐	☐	☐
Religious matters	☐	☐	☐	☐	☐	☐
Demonstrations of affection	☐	☐	☐	☐	☐	☐
Friends	☐	☐	☐	☐	☐	☐
Sex relations	☐	☐	☐	☐	☐	☐
Conventionality(correct or proper behaviour)	☐	☐	☐	☐	☐	☐
Philosophy of life	☐	☐	☐	☐	☐	☐
Ways of dealing with parents or in-laws	☐	☐	☐	☐	☐	☐
Aims, goals, and things believed important	☐	☐	☐	☐	☐	☐
Amount of time spent together	☐	☐	☐	☐	☐	☐
Making major decisions	☐	☐	☐	☐	☐	☐
Household tasks	☐	☐	☐	☐	☐	☐
Leisure time interests and activities	☐	☐	☐	☐	☐	☐
Career decisions	☐	☐	☐	☐	☐	☐
Other (please specify): _____	☐	☐	☐	☐	☐	☐
Other (please specify): _____	☐	☐	☐	☐	☐	☐

Activity 4.2 What are Our Conflict Patterns?

On the video you saw examples of different patterns of conflict management. **As a couple,** read through the patterns described below and rate which patterns apply to you as a couple. Note, you may use different patterns at different times.

Demand-withdraw	Escalate
When a problem arises in our relationship, one of us demands (tries to talk about the problem). Often the demander complains or criticises. The other person withdraws (talks little, may not listen, leaves the room, or refuses to discuss the issue).	When we talk about a problem, we tend to blame, attack, and criticise each other. We tend not to listen to each other, and things can get heated.
Does this pattern apply to you two? ☐ Almost all of the time ☐ Most of the time ☐ Sometimes ☐ Rarely ☐ Never	Does this pattern apply to you two? ☐ Almost all of the time ☐ Most of the time ☐ Sometimes ☐ Rarely ☐ Never
In demand-withdraw the demander often feels frustrated and not listened to. The withdrawer often feels attacked and may feel that talking achieves little. Demand-withdraw makes it difficult to understand each other or to solve problems.	When couples escalate, nasty fights can result. Often problems are unsolved, and partners often have hurt feelings.

Avoid	Effective Conflict Management
When there is a problem, we do not get around to talking, We put off discussing the problem.	When a problem arises we both talk about the problem. We hear each other out. We both suggest possible solutions and compromises.
Does this pattern apply to you two?	Does this pattern apply to you two?
☐ Almost all of the time	☐ Almost all of the time
☐ Most of the time	☐ Most of the time
☐ Sometimes	☐ Sometimes
☐ Rarely	☐ Rarely
☐ Never	☐ Never
Avoidance often means conflict is not obvious, but partners can become irritated and distant from each other. The problems are rarely solved. Avoidance can develop if there has been escalation in the past.	In effective conflict management both partners are active in the discussion. Both use effective listener and speaker skills. They usually feel that they can talk about and solve problems.

Managing Differences Well

You have looked at how you handle conflict now. Let's review the guidelines and ground rules for good conflict management from the video.

Guidelines for good conflict management

1. Do not try to solve the problem too quickly.

2. Take turns to listen and to speak. If this is hard to remember try to:

   - Use the floor technique

   - Give feedback when in the listener role

   - Ask for feedback when speaking

3. Use your communication skills

- Hear your partner out
- Avoid attacking, e.g. use 'I statements'.
- Describe specifics
- Attend and encourage
- Be assertive (but not aggressive)
- Sensitively express negatives

You might like to take a copy of the list below and stick it on the fridge as a reminder on conflict guidelines.

Conflict Guidelines

1. Don't try to solve the problem too quickly
2. Take turns speaking and listening
   - Use the Floor Technique
   - Give feedback when in listener role
   - Ask for feedback when in speaker role
3. Use your communication skills
   - Hear your partner out
   - Use I-Statements
   - Provide specific/ concrete descriptions of problem behaviour
   - Attend to and encourage each other
   - Make specific positive requests for change
   - Sensitively raise negatives

A POINT TO PONDER

Effective conflict managers try to understand everybody's needs when discussing a problem. Often there is a solution that meets everybody's needs. So you need first to seek to understand, and only then to seek solutions.

Activity 4.3 Ground Rules for good conflict management

Ground rules are agreed-upon ways of managing conflict. Below is a list of possible ground rules for handling conflict.

As a couple, discuss and mark which ground rules you think would help you two manage conflict. There are some suggestions, and there also is room to write your own ground rules.

Freedom to Raise Issues Any time Either of us can bring up an issue at any time. (As distinct from trying to find a good time and place to raise issues.)	☐ Yes ☐ No
Right to Reschedule A partner can say, 'This is not a good time'. This partner should set up a time to talk soon. (You need to decide what "soon" means. Some people like to set a 24-hour limit, others leave it for a little longer).	☐ Yes ☐ No Time limit ——————
Regular Relationship Meetings We will hold regular couple meetings when we are relaxed and alert.	☐ Yes ☐ No
Under Stress, Focus On the Immediate Issue Under stress, we deal with the immediate issue on the spot, then talk about the larger relationship issue later at our couple meeting or at a time we set.	☐ Yes ☐ No
Use of Problem Solving Sheet Sometimes we will use a written problem-solving sheet to help stay focused on the topic under discussion. (Note: a sample problem-solving sheet is shown on page 59).	☐ Yes ☐ No

Clear Agenda We can agree sometimes to discuss just one issue at a relationship meeting.	☐ Yes ☐ No
Understand then Solve When we are discussing a problem, we agree first to listen to each other about the other's view of the problem. Suggestions to solve the problem are made only after we understand each other's point of view.	☐ Yes ☐ No
Use of Stop If we start to become upset either one of us can call a brief 'stop'. This means taking a few minutes off, like a mini 'time-out'. The stop gives a few minutes to reflect, and to try to talk more calmly.	☐ Yes ☐ No
Use of Time Out If we start to become upset either one of us can call a 'time out'. The partner who calls the 'time out' will schedule a time soon to talk more, when he or she is feeling calmer.	☐ Yes ☐ No
Your Ground Rule (1): _____ _____	☐ Yes ☐ No
Your Ground Rule (2): _____ _____	☐ Yes ☐ No

Using a problem solving sheet

A problem-solving sheet can be used when you have a difficult problem to solve. An example layout for the sheet is shown on the page opposite. First, define the problem. Then write down each partner's point of view and a 'joint' point of view. The 'joint' point of view is the shared view of the problem that you both agree on. It may take some discussion to come up with a 'joint' point of view. Then generate some possible solutions to the problem. Next, think about the pros (positives) and cons (negatives) for each possible solution. Finally, choose the solution that best suits you as a couple.

Couple Problem Solving Sheet

• Define the issue (define clearly, specifically, positively):

Partner 1's point of view:_____

_____

_____

Partner 2's point of view:_____

_____

_____

Joint point of view:_____

_____

_____

• Possible Solutions	Pros (positives)	Cons (negatives)
1. _____	_____	_____
_____	_____	_____
2. _____	_____	_____
_____	_____	_____
3. _____	_____	_____
_____	_____	_____

• Solution decided upon: _____

_____

_____

Part B: Assessing and Improving Your Conflict Management

Activity 4.4 How are my conflict management skills now?

Now, let's look at how you are managing conflict now. This exercise is similar to the communication exercise in Unit 2. First, you have a discussion about a conflict topic.

For this exercise you will need:

• a watch or smart phone, and

• a quiet time and place

There are 4 steps in the exercise.

As a couple, choose a topic that you disagree about in your relationship. Choose a topic that has been a source of conflict. You might like to choose an area from the Areas of Diferences table on page 53.

Next, **on your own,** write down your personal goals for the discussion in the 'My Conflict Skills Goals' box below. You can use the checklist on the next page to help you choose your goals.

My Conflict Skills Goals

In my discussion with my partner about a topic of conflict, I have the following goal/s (be as specific as possible):

_____

_____

_____

As a couple, decide who will be the timekeeper. Talk for *three to four* minutes.

On your own, evaluate your conflict skills using the Conflict Skills Self-evaluation on the next page. This checklist contains the communication skills we covered in Unit 2 as well as other conflict skills from this unit.

Conflict Skills Self-Evaluation Form

Date:_____

On your own, place a tick in the appropriate box to describe how **you** think you went during the discussion using this key. (Remember, you won't necessarily use all these skills):

0	No use of this skill
1	Some use of this skill
2	OK, but could be better
3	Good use of this skill
N/A	Skill not applicable

SKILL	0	1	2	3	N/A
Conflict Skills					
I listened first before offering solutions	☐	☐	☐	☐	☐
I balanced listening and speaking to about equal time.	☐	☐	☐	☐	☐
Speaker Skills					
Described specifics	☐	☐	☐	☐	☐
Assertive	☐	☐	☐	☐	☐
Sensitively expressed negatives	☐	☐	☐	☐	☐
Self-disclosed feelings	☐	☐	☐	☐	☐
Listener Skills					
Attended	☐	☐	☐	☐	☐
Encouraged	☐	☐	☐	☐	☐
Summarised content	☐	☐	☐	☐	☐
Summarised feelings	☐	☐	☐	☐	☐
Asked question	☐	☐	☐	☐	☐
Heard my partner out	☐	☐	☐	☐	☐
Couple Ground Rules					
Used a written problem solving sheet	☐	☐	☐	☐	☐
We stayed with one agenda issue	☐	☐	☐	☐	☐
We used the floor technique to control speaking and listening roles.	☐	☐	☐	☐	☐
We called a time out, and rescheduled the discussion.	☐	☐	☐	☐	☐
We called a brief stop because it got heated, then started again.	☐	☐	☐	☐	☐
Other ground rule (write in):	☐	☐	☐	☐	☐

My strengths in managing conflict are:

_____

_____

_____

Things I need to work on managing conflict are:

_____

_____

_____

Activity 4.5 Partner Feedback Exercise

The next exercise is to swap feedback with your partner on the conflict management talk you just had.

On your own, identify two positives and one suggestion for change about the way **your partner** managed conflict.

1st Positive

_____

_____

2nd Positive

_____

_____

Suggestion for change:

_____

_____

_____

As a couple, discuss the feedback with your partner. Remember the communication guidelines from Unit 2 on giving suggestions for change and make sure you use your communication skills.

On your own, and based on your conflict skills self-evaluation and your partner's feedback, write down one aspect of your conflict management skills you think could be improved.

Part C Getting Back to Normal After a Conflict

Even couples that have well managed conflict sometimes get upset when discussing problems in their relationship. When conflict results in you feeling bad or upset it can take a while to get back to positive feelings. There are *four steps* you can use to re-establish positive feelings. The first three steps focus on thinking your way past negative feelings. The last step is reconnecting with your partner.

Step 1. Monitor your thoughts and feelings.

- After the conflict, be aware of your thoughts and feelings.

- Ask yourself : 'What thoughts are running through my head?' and 'What feelings do I have?'.

Step 2. Identify negative thoughts that make you upset or angry.

- Unhelpful thoughts are ones that keep you feeling sad or angry.

- Examples of unhelpful thoughts include: 'We are never going to resolve this' or 'He is never going to change'.

Step 3. Try to replace your negative thoughts with more helpful ones.

- Helpful thoughts calm you and help you focus on positive action you can take.

- Examples of helpful thoughts include: 'This will get resolved, just not this second' and 'People do change, but it takes time, and she needs to do it on her own' or 'We are not getting anywhere at this stage, what should I do differently?'

Step 4. Show positive feelings.

- Take action to show your positive feelings. Give your partner a hug, or say or do something positive in order to re-establish warmth.

Activity 4.6 How we recover after conflict

As a couple, discuss what usually happens after you two have an argument? Write down the positive things you have done in the past to recover after an argument. Note things you think you need to work on in order to recover better from arguments.

Recovering After Conflict

Positive things done in the past:

_____

_____

_____

Things to work on:

_____

_____

_____

Activity 4.7 Self-Change Plan

Now it is time to translate your reflections on this unit into action. Please complete the self-change plan over the page for one aspect of your conflict management you would like to change.

Self-Change Plan for Conflict

1. Describe

Choose an aspect of your conflict management you'd like to work on that involves changing something about your behaviour. Describe this aspect clearly and positively (write in the spaces provided).

_____

_____

_____

2. Focus

What do I currently do?

_____

_____

What are the **pluses** of my current behaviour?

_____

_____

What are the **minuses** of my current behaviour?

_____

_____

3. Set a Goal

Define exactly what I want to do. Where and when will I do it?

_____

_____

What might get in the way? How will I make sure it happens?

_____

_____

_____

4. Evaluate (Afterwards)

What did I actually do?

_____

_____

What **positives** resulted?

_____

_____

What **negatives** resulted?

_____

_____

What do I do from here?

_____

_____

I was wondering ...

Note down any questions, concerns, worries, thoughts, or ideas you have about Unit 4. Your relationship educator is available to discuss issues or answer questions.

_____

_____

_____

_____

_____

Sexual Intimacy

Overview

Aims of Unit 5

Part A   To explore your ideas about sex, and debunk some common myths about sex. 'What attitudes did my family of origin have when it came to sex?' 'How can I separate out the myths from the facts about sex?'

Part B   To assess and improve your communication about sex. 'Why can sex be hard to talk about?' 'What do we each like and dislike in sex?'

Part C   To review how you manage differences in sexual desire. 'We seem to have different levels of desire, what can we do?'

Part D   To explore how to keep sex satisfying. 'What can affect sexual interest?' 'How do we keep the 'zing'?'

Suggested Unit Activities

As you work through this unit the following activities will be suggested.

On your own   Reflect upon your early learning about sex through childhood, adolescence and early adulthood.

As a couple   Discuss common myths about sex, and how these myths can interfere with a good sex life.

As a couple   Review how you talk about sex.

As a couple   Discuss how to sustain sexual satisfaction in the long term.

On your own   Develop a self-change plan to strengthen your relationship.

A Special Note. Sex is very private for most people. Your relationship educator has been trained to deal sensitively and confidentially with the topic of sex. He or she is happy to talk openly with you about sex in your relationship. However, your privacy will be respected. Please feel free to decline to talk about aspects of your sex life that you do not feel comfortable talking about.

Reflecting on Unit 4...

Think about what you did in Unit 4 — Managing Conflict. Write down any ideas that you liked. How have you used these ideas since doing Unit 3 (even if only in a small way)?

Ideas I liked:

_____

_____

_____

How I have used the ideas:

_____

_____

_____

How did you go carrying out your self-change plan from Unit 1?

_____

_____

_____

Circle the number that best describes how far you went in doing your self-change plan.

very poor/ did not do anything					OK, did try				excellent did it all	
0	1	2	3	4	5	6	7	8	9	10

Part A: Early Learning About Sex

Early learning shapes much of our ideas about sex. It can affect our current sex life in lots of ways.

The people who cared for us when we were young (usually our parents) have a big influence on our views about sex. These family-of-origin experiences shape how we think sex should be.

What our friends say about sex also gives us ideas about sex. For example, we may pick up ideas about how often others have sex, or what things they do during sex.

Previous sexual experiences also shape your ideas. Most people have relationships with other people before making a commitment to their current partner. You might have had a range of dating partners, have lived with someone, or married someone before meeting your current partner.

In this exercise you are asked to write down your personal thoughts and feelings. These are your own private thoughts and you may prefer to keep these to yourself. It is important that you and your partner each respect the other's privacy. Do not feel you have to talk to each other about these issues if you do not want to. Of course, if you are comfortable talking about what is on these pages; please do so with your partner.

Often messages about sex that we learn are subtle. For example, how would (did) your parents have reacted if one of them accidentally walked in when you were masturbating as a teenager? How did you get the message that they would have been angry or embarrassed or accepting or whatever?

Activity 5.1 Your memories and thoughts about sex

On your own, read the examples of other people's recollections and thoughts about sex in the box over the page and then write down your own thoughts about the questions posed.

Childhood

What did your parents, and any brothers or sisters communicate to you about sex. Did they talk about sex much? Did they talk about sex positively or negatively?

_____

_____

_____

_____

_____

_____

'Early on I learned about sex from my older sisters — it was something naughty and exotic — my sisters called it 'the deed'. I guess I thought sex was something good but you didn't talk about it or you would get into trouble. I still find it a bit hard to talk about with my partner, even though he is very open about it. It's something I'm working on'.
Lee, 33, married 3 years to Robin, 29.

'My dad didn't want to talk to me about sex. He just suggested I look at porn. I thought that sex was only for the beautiful. I felt ashamed of how I looked, and anxious about being naked in front of a woman. I felt like a dismal failure as a man. Later on I worked out I wasn't the only one who felt that way'.
Leong, 34.

'I had a girlfriend who told me you wouldn't get pregnant if you did it standing up. But she was always in the back of some bloke's car, so I couldn't see how she could stand up.'
Natalie

'My first time was with a girl I barely knew. We both were really drunk. I remember thinking 'is that it?' Then I threw up. Not real romantic.'
Toby

Adolescence

What was your parents' attitude towards you and sex in your teenage years? Were they strict? Easy going? Punishing?

_____

_____

_____

What about friends? Did you see yourself as more or less sexually active than your friends? What was the craziest thing anyone ever tried to tell you about sex?

_____

_____

_____

Other Experiences

How other experiences influenced your attitudes to sex? How have you decided what is OK/Not OK for you?

_____

_____

_____

_____

'Paolo is sensitive to my likes and dislikes. He is OK and does not take it personally if I don't feel like sex. Being with him has made me a more demanding lover; I never used to start sex before. Now I do. And I ask what he likes. Which made me a better lover too? At least I hope so!'
Natasha, 54, partner to Paolo, 52, for four years.

Today

What attitudes do you have now that helps your sex life with your partner?

_____

_____

_____

What attitudes (if any) do you have now that does not help your sex life with your partner?

_____

_____

_____

As a couple, talk to each other about what you have written down that you wish to share with your partner. Focus in particular on the positive things you bring to your sexual relationship.

A POINT TO PONDER

Ideally, how often do you think you and your partner should have sex? What do you think shapes your idea of how often you should have sex?

Part B: Common Myths About Sex

Ideas about sex and relationships are shown to us every day online, on television, in movies, newspapers and magazines. Stories of beautiful celebrities bedding each other appear all the time. Photographs of perfect looking sports stars, models and actors (with not a hair out place) fill web sites and popular magazines. These celebrities and their relationships are shown as the ideals of being sexy and successful.

The view of the celebrity sex life we get from the media is nonsense. No one looks good all the time. No one feels sexy all the time. Some days we are tired, or feel ill.

It is easy for people to feel that you have to be slim, young, rich and beautiful to be sexy or have a good relationship.

In contrast to the hype surrounding celebrity relationships, most people are very private about the realities of their sexual relationship. Given the absence of real information about real relationships, many people start to believe that what is shown in the media is accurate. The myths about sex can lead people to worry about aspects of their sex lives. Getting our facts right can help. Listed below are a few important myths about sex, along with the realities. You can read them through first on their own and then talk about them together.

Activity 5.2 Exploring sexual myths

On your own, read through the myths listed below. Put a mark beside any myths you think you struggle with. Then **as a couple**, discuss the myths, and what you think about them.

Myth 1: Sex is all about orgasms.

Reality check: Sex does not have to be just about reaching orgasm. Sex is about lots of things. Sex can be relaxing and sensual without having an orgasm. Sex can be about giving pleasure to your partner. Sex can be expressing how you feel.

For most women orgasm does not occur every time they have sex. In fact, only one-third of women say they reach climax from intercourse 'most of the time'. Another third of women say they reach orgasm 'some of the time', and a third say they 'rarely or never' reach orgasm during intercourse.

Most men do reach orgasm most of the time with intercourse. But it is common for men not to reach orgasm from time to time.

There is no correct or normal way to be. If you are satisfied with your current sex life and how often you achieve orgasm, then that is fine. If you are not satisfied, there are things you can try to enhance your sexual enjoyment. Your relationship educator can give you advice.

Myth 2: Love making should be great 100% of the time.

Reality check: In all relationships sex varies. More than likely sometimes sex will be great, sometimes just OK, and much of the time sex will be pretty good. Sex tends to better more of the time in relationships when the couple:

- do their best to stay fit and healthy

- spend time on being romantic and having special couple time

- make time for sex to be leisurely

- the relationship as a whole is working well

Myth 3: My body should be perfect in order to have a good sex life.

Reality check: Most models look rotten in the morning. The glamour seen online and in magazines is a fake. The images look so good because of good lighting and make up, and then most images are edited to remove faults. No one has the perfect looks.

A good sex life usually means we need to accept how we look. If you hate your body or how it looks, it can be hard to have a good sex life. If you feel uncomfortable with how you look naked, talk this over with your relationship educator.

Myth 4: Only intercourse is real sex.

Reality check: Happy couples tend to have a wide variety of sexual and sensual things they do together. Sometimes a cuddle, massage or petting can be fun and can express sexual feelings without intercourse.

There are times when options other than intercourse can be good. Some couples like oral sex or mutual masturbation for variety.

Sometimes intercourse is not a good option. For example, some couples dislike intercourse when the woman has her period. For a period after childbirth, sex may be uncomfortable for the woman. At such times other forms of sex, such as mutual touching, can be good.

Myth 5: If your relationship is good, you should both feel like sex at the same time.

Reality Check: Everyone varies in how sexy they feel. Everyone has days when they are too tired, or just do not feel that way. So it is impossible for two partners to always desire sex at the same time.

It is important that the couple find ways of signalling to each other when they do feel like sex. And it is important to respect when your partner does not feel like sex.

If one partner does not feel like sex at a particular time, masturbation can provide release. Most people do masturbate from time to time.

Myth 6: Impotence is always a sign of serious problems.

Reality Check: Impotence is the inability to get or keep an erection during sex. Many men are impotent from time to time. Sometimes impotence is caused by a clear medical problem. Other times psychological factors can cause impotence. For example, stress and too much to drink can cause impotence. If impotence is causing problems in your relationship talk to a doctor. Many impotence problems can now be treated.

Myth 7: Men come too fast and women too slowly.

Reality check: Individuals vary greatly in how quickly they become aroused, and by what. It is common for men to achieve orgasm during intercourse more quickly than women, but this varies from time to time and from couple to couple.

Try to make sure that sex occurs when both partners are interested. Foreplay needs to be arousing for both partners. This requires letting each other know what is pleasurable. If there are differences in how quickly each of you reaches orgasm, and if this is a problem in your relationship, talk to your relationship educator.

Part C: Talking About Sex

Before we begin ...

The following two exercises are mainly for couples who have had sex together. Some people doing this program might not have had sex with their partner. (For example, some engaged couples decide to start sex after they are married). If you have not had sex with your partner, focus your discussion on how you want your sex life to be in the future. We suggest you return to discuss the issues in this chapter again when you are having sex together.

Communicating about sex

One key to a satisfying sex life is **good sexual communication**. Two sex topics that many couples talk about quite a bit are: how often they have sex, and how they have sex.

How Often We Have Sex

In all relationships there are times when one person wants to have sex and the other person does not. In some couples this is accepted. The couple talks about how often to have sex. In other couples differences in desire for sex can become a problem. The person who wants to have sex can feel hurt and rejected. The person who does not want sex can feel pressured and resentful.

Each partner's sex drive is likely to change over time. Influences such as illness, pregnancy, changes in working hours, or stress at home or work, can all affect sex drive. This means that working out how often you have sex is not something you can agree on for the future. You have to keep working out your sex life as you go.

Activity 5.3 How often we have sex and how we feel about it.

On your own, place a tick in the square that best answers each question.

1. Over the last few months we have had sex:

6–7 days per week	☐
3–5 days per week	☐
once or twice per week	☐
every 2 to 3 weeks	☐
once per month or less	☐

2. How often we have had sex over the last few months is

       Much more often than I like ☐

       A little bit more often than I like ☐

       About right ☐

       A bit less often than I like ☐

       Much less often than I would like ☐

3. Who initiates sex in your relationship?

       Me, most of the time we have sex ☐

       Both of us, but me more often ☐

       Both of us, about equally ☐

       Both of us, but my partner more often ☐

       My partner, most of the time we have sex. ☐

4. When you do initiate sex with your partner, what do you say or do?

_____

_____

_____

5. When your partner initiates sex with you, what does he or she say or do?

_____

_____

_____

As a couple discuss your answers. Write down your thoughts about how you negotiate how often you have sex.

Strengths about how we decide how often to have sex:

_____

_____

_____

Areas to work on:

_____

_____

_____

If one partner consistently wants sex more often than the other. This can happen in relationships. Most often it is the man wanting sex more often than the woman, but it is not always that way.

Sometimes one partner rarely, if ever, feels like sex. If you have lost most of your interest in sex, you might want to talk that over with your relationship educator. There are ways to improve sexual interest.

If you both feel like sex at least sometimes, there can still be a difference in how often you feel like sex. To help manage this issue, you might want to try some of the following (as suggested on the video).

- Talk about it. This is probably best done not in bed, but at a quiet time.

- If you're the one saying 'no', try a 'maybe' sometimes (but do not feel like sex is a duty you must do).

- Say 'no' nicely.

- If you're the one initiating always accept 'no'.

- If you initiate a lot, back off a little. Give your partner more chance to initiate when they are in the mood.

- If you initiate little, try asking for sex more often, when you feel most like it.

How We Have Sex

Partners are unlikely to always agree on what sexual activities they like. This is normal. In a good relationship, the partners clearly tell each other what they do and do not like. In that way, the couple can experiment, while never forcing someone to do things they really dislike.

'I always really loved having sex standing up but I was aware that he wasn't as keen on it as I was. One day I asked about it and he told me that it was quite hard on his back. We experimented a little bit and found out that if I stood on something it was much more enjoyable.' Anna.

Activity 5.4 Sexual Likes and Dislikes Form

In the following exercise you reflect on your sexual likes and dislikes. The idea is to know what you like, and make sure you have sex with your partner in ways you enjoy and feel comfortable with.

A POINT TO PONDER

Do you have particularly strong sexual turn-ons or turn-offs? Are there any particular experiences that gave you those strong feelings?

On your own, place a tick in the appropriate box in the form below.

Sexual Preferences Form

Activity	It's pretty good as it is	It's OK but we could make it better	Haven't done this but would like to try it	Don't want to do this
Initiating sex with my partner	☐	☐	☐	☐
Having my partner initiate sex	☐	☐	☐	☐
Kissing each other for more than one minute	☐	☐	☐	☐
Telling my partner my fantasies	☐	☐	☐	☐
Having my partner tell me his/her fantasies	☐	☐	☐	☐
Giving my partner a non-genital massage	☐	☐	☐	☐
Receiving a non-genital massage	☐	☐	☐	☐
Caressing my partner's nipples/ other non-genital area he/she finds stimulating with my hands or lips Area: _____	☐	☐	☐	☐
Having my partner caress my nipples/ other non-genital area with her/ his hands or lips Area: _____	☐	☐	☐	☐

Activity	It's pretty good as it is	It's OK but we could make it better	Haven't done this but would like to try it	Don't want to do this
Caressing my partner's genitals with my hands	☐	☐	☐	☐
Having my partner caress my genitals with his/ her hands	☐	☐	☐	☐
Giving my partner oral sex	☐	☐	☐	☐
Receiving oral sex from my partner	☐	☐	☐	☐
Giving and receiving oral sex simultaneously with my partner	☐	☐	☐	☐
Watching my partner masturbate	☐	☐	☐	☐
Having my partner watch me masturbate	☐	☐	☐	☐
Mutual masturbation	☐	☐	☐	☐
Having intercourse in the following positions	☐	☐	☐	☐
1. _____	☐	☐	☐	☐
2. _____	☐	☐	☐	☐
3. _____	☐	☐	☐	☐
4. _____	☐	☐	☐	☐
Having anal sex	☐	☐	☐	☐
Using sex toys to stimulate my partner	☐	☐	☐	☐
Having my partner use sex toys to stimulate me	☐	☐	☐	☐
Having sex away from home	☐	☐	☐	☐
Having dress-up/ role-play sex	☐	☐	☐	☐
Other: _____	☐	☐	☐	☐
Other: _____	☐	☐	☐	☐

Sexual strengths and areas to work on

On your own, answer the questions below. Then, **as a couple,** discuss your answers.

On your own, write down two strengths or things you really like about how you currently have sex with your partner. Then write down one thing you would like to work on.

Strength 1:

_____

_____

_____

Strength 2:

_____

_____

_____

Area to work on:

_____

_____

_____

Now, **as a couple,** discuss your answers.

Sex is sometimes hard to talk about, so you might like to consider the following tips for communicating well about sex.

• Use the communication skills you learned in Unit 2.

• Be sensitive to your partner's feelings. This means listening to your partner's feelings, and choosing your own words carefully. Many people feel vulnerable when talking about sex, so pleased be gentle and loving with each other.

- If you would like something to change, make suggestions, not demands.
- Be very specific when you tell your partner what you like.
- Ask your partner specifically what he/she likes.

Part D: Keeping Sex Satisfying

One challenge in a long-term relationship is to keep sex satisfying. Some couples find their sex life becomes a bit bland or boring.

Your satisfaction with your sex life might vary because of influences outside your relationship. These influences might have a negative or a positive effect. For example, being tired or stressed after starting a new job may decrease your enjoyment of sex. Having a short break away together might kindle some romance and improve sex.

Activity 5.5 Managing challenges to your sex life

As a couple, fill out the table below. Try to identify two things that might happen that could impact upon your sex life. Write down how you can increase the positive effects and decrease the negative effects of influences on your sex life.

Things that may impact on our sex life	What is the likely effect? (Be specific)	How can we increase positives and decrease negative effects?
Example Mark has been offered a great new job. If he accepts, he will be out of town every second week for 3–4 days.	Mark and Shan will have less time together overall, and less time for sex.	Could reject job. If accept job: Plan couple nights 2–3 nights per week when Mark is home. Plan lots of telephone calls while Mark is away so they can flirt on the phone. Plan romantic weekends once every six weeks.

Activity 5.6 A Sexuality Self-Change Plan

In this Unit we have reviewed sexual learning, sexual myths, how often you have sex, how you have sex and how to sustain your sexual satisfaction. **On your own** complete a self-change plan over the page to improve any aspect of your sex life that you would like to focus upon.

Self-Change Plan for Sexuality

1. Describe	2. Focus
Choose an issue in your sex life you'd like to work on that involves changing something about your behaviour. Describe this aspect clearly and positively (write in the spaces provided).	What do I currently do?
_____ _____ _____ _____	_____ _____ What are the **pluses** of my current behaviour? _____ _____ What are the **minuses** of my current behaviour? _____ _____

3. Set a Goal	4. Evaluate (Afterwards)
Define exactly what I want to do. Where and when will I do it? _____ _____ _____ What might get in the way? How will I make sure it happens? _____ _____ _____	What did I actually do? _____ _____ What **positives** resulted? _____ _____ What **negatives** resulted? _____ _____ What do I do from here? _____ _____

I was wondering ...

Note down any questions, concerns, worries, thoughts, or ideas you have about Unit 5. Your relationship educator is available to discuss issues or answer questions.

_____

_____

_____

_____

_____

Looking Ahead

Overview

Aims of Unit

Part A   To help you develop good mutual support for each other in your relationship. 'How can I help when my partner is stressed or upset? Sometimes I seem to make things worse, what should I do?'

Part B   To explore likely changes that will occur in your life, and how they may impact upon your relationship.

Part C   To suggest some early warning signs of relationship challenges and options for getting things back on track.

Part D   To help you develop ways to keep your relationship a priority in your life.

Suggested Activities

As you work through this unit the following activities will be suggested.

As a couple   Review your skills in being supportive of each other.

As a couple   Reflect on possible changes in your life, and how such changes would impact on your relationship.

As a couple   Plan strategies that will help you to adapt to life changes.

As a couple   Consider early warning signs that might indicate your relationship is getting off track, and how you could refocus on your relationship if needed.

On your own   Review your relationship vision now that you have nearly finished CoupleCARE.

As a couple   Consider ways to keep your relationship happy across along life together.

Reflecting on Unit 5...

Think about what you did in Unit 5 — Sexual Intimacy. Write down any ideas that you liked. How have you applied these ideas since you did unit 5 (even if only in a small way)?

Ideas I liked:

_____

_____

_____

How I have used the ideas:

_____

_____

_____

How did you go carrying out your self-change plan from Unit 1?

_____

_____

_____

_____

Circle the number that best describes how far you went in doing your self-change plan.

very poor/ did not do anything					OK, did try				excellent did it all	
0	1	2	3	4	5	6	7	8	9	10

Part A: Giving Support

The support partners provide for each other makes a big difference to how well each copes with stress. Mutual support strengthens the relationship.
There are three types of support we can show our partners.

1. *Emotion-focused support* is listening, showing understanding, and helping *your partner to open up about a problem.*

2. *Problem-focused support* is helping your partner to find solutions to a problem.

3. *Practical support* is doing things to help your partner. It might be doing an extra chore to help them when she or he is busy at work, or getting them a small gift to support a hobby or favourite activity.

Emotion-Focused Support

Often when people feel stressed they want someone to listen to them. They might not want or need a solution to a problem, they just want to feel understood and supported. Emotion-focused support is useful when your partner just wants you to listen.

When offering emotion-focused support you try to UNDERSTAND your partner's feelings and thoughts. You do NOT try to give solutions, advice, or your own opinion.

In Emotion-Focused Support you:

- Help your partner express their feelings.

- Attend, encourage, ask questions and paraphrase your partner's feelings.

- Offer affection with touch, hugs.

Problem-Focused Support

Sometimes when people are stressed by a problem they find it hard to work out what to do. In problem-focused support you can help your partner to find solutions to the problem.

In Problem-Focused Support you:

- Help your partner define the problem.

- Suggest a specific plan of action.

- Offer your partner specific assistance.

Practical support

Practical support is doing things that help your partner — particularly important in times of stress. For example, you might cook an extra meal to reduce the load on your partner if work is busy for them; or you might suggest you pick the children up from school or day care so your partner can visit a sick friend or relative; or offer to go with your partner to a doctor's appointment if your partner is worried about her health.

In order to provide the most helpful practical support for your partner, you need to know what is happening in their life. You can only do this well if you have regular conversations in which you show real interest in each other's world. It also builds your knowledge of what is going on in your partner's life. Then, when they have a problem, you are better able to support them.

In Practical support you:

• Regularly ask your partner about their day, and what is coming up for them.

• You offer to do things that might help your partner when they are stressed.

• You ask if there are things you can do that would support your partner in their interests.

So which type of support is best?

Different types of support are needed at different times. It is important to be able to shift from one kind of support to another as the need arises.
If you're not sure what kind of support your partner wants in a situation:

1. Ask your partner what type of support he/she would like. You might say: 'Do you want to just talk about this or do you want to look for solutions?' 'Is there anything I can do to help you with this?'

2. Notice how your partner responds to your support efforts in different situations, and fine tune what support you provide.

3. Ask your partner for feedback on the type of support you provide. For example, you might ask 'Was that the kind of support you wanted? What would you have liked?'

Having reflected on the three types of support, **on your own** write down any new ideas for you have for offering your partner support.

_____

_____

_____

Activity 6.1 How am I going at support?

This exercise is similar to the communication exercise in Unit 2, and the conflict management exercise in Unit 4. We want you to have a discussion together and review your communication. Except this time the focus is on how each of you support each other during a discussion.

For this exercise you will need:

- a watch or smart phone, and

- a quiet time and place

Here's what you do.

On your own choose a topic to discuss and write it in the space provided below. Chose something you would like to _change about yourself_ as an individual, so your partner can practise showing you support. Choose something that does not cause tension in your relationship. It can be an important personal characteristic, problem, or issue you would like to change about yourself (e.g., wanting to get fit, dealing with stress at work).

My topic to discuss is:

_____

_____

On your own decide what goals you have for showing your partner support. Write your goals in the space provided below. (Remember to keep your goals to just a couple of points — it's easier that way.)

_____

_____

My Support Goals

Based on what I have already learned during this unit about support, in my discussion with my partner I have the following goal(s) for my support skills (be as specific as possible):

_____

_____

_____

_____

Next, **as a couple** appoint one of you to keep track of the time. Decide on whose topic you will talk about first. Spend three minutes talking about the first topic, then swap around. When it's your partner's turn to discuss his/her topic, practice the support skills from this unit, and keep in mind your goals for the discussion.

On you own evaluate your support skills using the Relationship Support Skills Checklist on the facing page.

A POINT TO PONDER

What is the most important way someone has supported you? What did they do? What made that support so helpful to you?

Relationship Support Skills Checklist

On your own, place a tick in the appropriate box to rate your support skills (Remember, you won't necessarily use all these skills in your discussion):

0	No use of this skill
1	Some use of this skill
2	OK, but could be better
3	Good use of this skill
N/A	Skill not applicable

SKILL	0	1	2	3	N/A
Speaker Skills					
Described specifics	☐	☐	☐	☐	☐
Assertive	☐	☐	☐	☐	☐
Sensitively expressed negatives	☐	☐	☐	☐	☐
Self-disclosed feelings	☐	☐	☐	☐	☐
Listener Skills					
Attended	☐	☐	☐	☐	☐
Encouraged	☐	☐	☐	☐	☐
Summarised content	☐	☐	☐	☐	☐
Summarised feelings	☐	☐	☐	☐	☐
Asked question	☐	☐	☐	☐	☐
Heard my partner out	☐	☐	☐	☐	☐
Emotion-focused support					
Helped partner express feelings	☐	☐	☐	☐	☐
Encouraged, reassured, gave affection	☐	☐	☐	☐	☐
Problem-focused support					
Helped define the problem	☐	☐	☐	☐	☐
Suggested specific plan of action	☐	☐	☐	☐	☐
Offered specific assistance	☐	☐	☐	☐	☐
Practical support					
Asked what I could do to help was needed	☐	☐	☐	☐	☐
Suggested something I could do to help	☐	☐	☐	☐	☐

My strengths in the communication:

_____

_____

_____

Things I need to work on in communication:

_____

_____

_____

Partner Feedback on Support

On your own, based on the support discussion, note down two positives about the way your partner showed you support.

As a couple, give each other feedback about how you provided support.

First Positive:

_____

Second Positive:

_____

Now, note down one suggestion for improvement in the way your partner supports you. (Be specific and positive):

_____

_____

As a couple, discuss the feedback with your partner. Remember the guidelines from Unit 2, page 23 on giving feedback. After giving each other some feedback, and **based on your partner's feedback,** write down some specific strengths and weaknesses of your support of your partner.

Strengths:

_____

_____

Areas to work on:

_____

_____

Your relationship educator will review the self-evaluation you have done, and explore the feedback you received from your partner. If you have specific areas you want to work on in supporting your partner, you might like to complete a self-change plan on support. There is a blank self-change plan at the end of this unit.

Part B: Managing Change

A POINT TO PONDER

In a healthy relationship the couple adapts to change in ways that help their relationship. Reflecting on your parent's relationship, what was the biggest change they had to adapt to in their relationship? How well do you think they adapted?

Every relationship goes through changes. Some changes might be planned, such as getting married, moving cities to take a job, or having a child. Other changes can just happen, such as losing a job, becoming ill, or having a child. (Yes, we did say that — having a child can be planned or just happen.)

Some changes may help your relationship. Some changes may not help. Some common changes that happen to couples are listed below. You will have some control over the changes that happen, so think about what you would like by way of change.

Activity 6.2 Identifying likely changes in our life together

As a couple, place a tick in the boxes below beside those changes you think *are more likely than not* to happen to you in the next *2 years*. If you think the change is unlikely to occur in the next 2 years, then consider if those same changes *are more likely than not* to happen in the next *10 years*.

Likely Changes in Our Life Together

Change	Within 2 years?	Within 10 years?
One partner changing to a different job	☐	☐
More responsibility at work	☐	☐
Change home within same city/area	☐	☐
Change home to a new city/area	☐	☐
A partner finishing a course or other training	☐	☐
A partner starting a course or other training	☐	☐

Birth of a child	☐	☐
A relative needing special care	☐	☐
Major purchase, (e.g. home or business)	☐	☐
A partner staying home from paid work	☐	☐
A major change in social activities	☐	☐
A major change in sporting activities	☐	☐
A major change in artistic activities	☐	☐
Retirement	☐	☐
One of our parents having health problems	☐	☐
Other: _____	☐	☐
Other: _____	☐	☐

To manage changes well it is useful to consider:

- the direct effects of the change,

- how the effects could impact on your relationship, and

- how you could manage those relationship effects.

Let's look at a hypothetical example.

Example of Planning for Change

John and Fong-Yi are preparing for Fong-Yi to begin full-time work next month. Fong-Yi has not worked outside the home since she and John have been together. They are thinking that the change will be quite hard to get used to so they have drawn up the table over the page to help them manage that change.

Direct effects of change	Possible effects on our relationship	Our plan to deal with relationship effects
1. Fong-Yi will have less time to attend to cleaning and cooking	1. If Fong-Li kept doing all her current chores plus work she might feel resentful. John may find it hard to get used to doing more of the chores.	1. We need to develop new routines for getting chores done. We need to agree on who does what. We need to talk this one through.
2. We'll have more money	2. We'll be able to save or spend money differently.	2. We could spend our money in lots of ways (e.g. save for a mortgage, get a cleaner to help with chores). We need to agree on our priorities and agree on a budget. Organise for cleaners to come in each week.
3. Fong-Yi will probably be more tired than now, she may need time to adjust to the demands of her new job.	3. Fong-Yi might feel the need for support from John.	3. John will take care to have regular couple time to talk to Fong-Li.
4. We will both be busier.	4. Having less time to talk may result in us being more stressed with each other.	4. Both of us to remember that this is a time of change and may be stressful at first. We need to have a regular date to have fun.

Activity 6.3   Managing changes in our life together

As a couple, from the list you completed earlier on page 98 —'Likely Changes in Our Life Together', — choose two changes that are likely to occur in the next two years. Complete one of the tables that follow for each of these two changes.

Planning for Change

Change (1) _____

Direct effects of change	Possible effects on our relationship	Our plan to deal with relationship effects

Planning for Change

Change (2) _____

Direct effects of change	Possible effects on our relationship	Our plan to deal with relationship effects

Of course, not all changes can be predicted ahead of time. When we are faced with an unexpected change or stress, well-practised relationship skills are a big help. The skills you've learned during CoupleCARE — including communication, support, caring, and conflict management — will help.

Part C: Early Warning Signs of Losing the Relationship Focus

Sometimes couple relationships get off track. Becoming busy with other things, feeling stressed, caring for your young child, or getting ill might lead you to reduce your relationship focus. There are many possible warning signs that your relationship is getting off track. Warning signs are small changes in how you and your partner relate. For example:

- You might be spending less quality time with your partner.

- The little acts of caring toward each other are less frequent.

- You are doing less fun activities together.

- You might be terse in how you speak to your partner.

- You are having sex less often.

- You are not finding time to talk to each other.

If you notice warning signs, it is important to attempt to correct things as soon as you notice.

Activity 6.4 Early Warning Signs

Even if you are very happy with your relationship, it can be helpful to identify behaviours or feelings that are early warning signs for things starting to go off track in your relationship.

On your own, look at the example below then, over the page, write down some early warning signs that might show up in your relationship if it were getting off track. Then write down some actions you might take if such warning signs occurred in your relationship. **As a couple** discuss what you have written down. What can you do to monitor early warning signs and maintain your focus on having a great relationship.

Early Warning Sign	What I might do
Example: My partner and I start arguing more than usual.	• Revisit the program materials, refresh our conflict management skills. • Talk about seeking couple therapy.

Early Warning Sign	What I might do

Part D: Maintaining a Relationship Focus

We hope that throughout CoupleCARE you have focused on your relationship on a day-to-day basis. If your relationship is to be as good as it possibly can be, it is important to continue this relationship focus. But how can we remember to focus on our relationship in the future? Life can be busy, and it is easy to let things slide.

A major risk for couples is that they start to take each other or the relationship for granted. It is easy to get caught up in your job, friends, family and other activities. These are all important aspects of your life. But your relationship needs to be central to your life if it is to flourish. There are two important things you can do to focus on your relationship for the long-term.

1. Review your relationship vision.

2. Maintain your use of relationship skills.

> **SOME POINTS TO PONDER ABOUT LONG-TERM COUPLES.**
>
> **One-third of all couples report they have not been on a date (going out, just the two of them) in the last 3 months.**
>
> **The average man with children speaks to his children for about 5 minutes per day, and to his wife for 10 minutes per day. The same man will watch about 2 hours of television per day.**

Activity 6.5 Reviewing Your Relationship vision

A regular review of your relationship vision will help you to keep working on how you want your relationship to be. Let's do your first review now.

Look back at the personal relationship vision you did in Unit 1 (pages 5 and 6). Since then you have spent some weeks thinking about your relationship. Is there anything you'd like to take out or change about your relationship vision? Are there any new ideas you would like to add to your vision? In particular, is there anything about how you will keep working on your relationship?

On your own, write down any changes you would like to make to your relationship vision. (Try to be as concrete as possible.)

_____

_____

_____

_____

As a couple, discuss your individual ideas about your relationship vision. Write down below the ideas you agree upon. It is not important if your individual relationship visions do not match exactly. What is important is that you agree on some ideas of how you want your relationship to be.

Our Shared Relationship Vision

_____

_____

_____

_____

Together you have just painted a word picture of how you want your relationship, your life together to be.

A Key Point to Remember

Over the years, it will be helpful to look over your relationship vision together. Ask yourselves at these times: Are we on track? Are there things we need to add or change? This way, you'll keep working towards achieving your hopes, dreams and plans for your relationship. Some couples use anniversaries, the new year, or other regular times to review their relationship.

Keep Using Your Relationship Skills

'Use it or lose it.' That is how many people describe hanging on to skills that you learn. Relationship skills need to be used, or they disappear.

Activity 6.6 Practicing what you have learned

On your own, think back over the past 5 units: self-change, communication, intimacy, managing differences, and sex. (To remind you of some of the skills covered in CoupleCARE, see the Relationship Support Skills Checklist on page 95).

Write down five things from CoupleCARE you liked and want to keep doing

1. _____

2. _____

3. _____

4. _____

5. _____

It's important to turn the skills you have learned from CoupleCARE into habits. Here are some ideas for consolidating these habits.

1. Make time to reflect and work actively on your relationship vision, your communication skills, support and caring skills, sexual intimacy skills, and to mix your shared and individual activities.

2. Occasionally (or regularly) dig out your CoupleCARE materials, watch the video and read over your guidebooks again.

3. Make a regular 'couple time' where you discuss your ongoing skills. This will help keep an ongoing dialogue between you and your partner about your relationship skills.

4. Remember to keep using self-change principles: continually work at changing your own behaviour in order to improve your relationship.

Skills I Will Try to Maintain

Following on pages 108 and 109 is the Couple CARE Relationship Skill Checklist. This checklist lists some of the important skills you've learned during the program. As a couple look through the checklist. Think about three skills that each of you will focus on doing for the next month.

As a couple select three skills that each of you will try to focus on in the next month.

1. _____

2. _____

3. _____

CoupleCare Relationship Skills Checklist

Skills	Date	Date	Date
Self-Change			
Review relationship vision	☐	☐	☐
Use 4-step self-change plan	☐	☐	☐
Communication			
Describe specifics	☐	☐	☐
Express positives	☐	☐	☐
Sensitively raise negatives	☐	☐	☐
Self-disclose feelings	☐	☐	☐
Attend	☐	☐	☐
Encourage	☐	☐	☐
Summarise content	☐	☐	☐
Summarise feelings	☐	☐	☐
Ask questions	☐	☐	☐
Hear my partner out	☐	☐	☐
Intimacy and Caring			
Showing day-to-day acts of caring	☐	☐	☐
Keep novelty and variety in caring behaviours	☐	☐	☐
Add more/new independent activities	☐	☐	☐
Add more/new couple activities	☐	☐	☐
Celebrate the relationship	☐	☐	☐

Skills	Date	Date	Date
Conflict management			
Don't try to solve the problem too quickly	☐	☐	☐
Use the floor technique	☐	☐	☐
When listening, give feedback	☐	☐	☐
When speaking, ask for feedback	☐	☐	☐
Hear my partner out	☐	☐	☐
Use 'I' statements	☐	☐	☐
Attend and encourage	☐	☐	☐
Describe problems specifically	☐	☐	☐
Make specific positive requests for change	☐	☐	☐
Use temporary stop	☐	☐	☐
Use time out	☐	☐	☐
Hold relationship meetings	☐	☐	☐
Sex			
Expressing preferences	☐	☐	☐
Balancing responsibility for initiating	☐	☐	☐
Support			
Emotion-focused support			
Help partner express feelings	☐	☐	☐
Encourage, reassure, give affection	☐	☐	☐
Problem-focused support			
Help define the problem	☐	☐	☐
Suggest specific plan of action	☐	☐	☐
Practical Support			
Offer partner specific assistance	☐	☐	☐
Ask what sort of support is needed	☐	☐	☐
Maintain a Relationship Focus			
Planning for change	☐	☐	☐
Review this checklist	☐	☐	☐

So that's how you can make sure you practise your CoupleCARE skills. But there are also ways you can keep working on *new* relationship skills into the future. You can ask yourself: 'What can we do? Where else can we go?'. Some ways to answer these questions are:

- Continually be on the lookout for new ways to develop your relationship skills and for sources of relationship insight.

- Attend workshops advertised in the paper, read books (ask for the self-help or psychology section in bookshops or in libraries).

- If you are having difficulties in your relationship, address these early. Many people nowadays go to couple counselling to do further work on their relationship. Of course, you can always go to a counsellor as an individual to talk about relationship issues too.

Activity 6.7 A Final Reflection

You have now worked through Units 1–6 of CoupleCARE — the whole program.

As a couple, reflect on program and write down what you liked and what you might find useful in the future.

_____

_____

_____

_____

Feeling good about our efforts is very important. Overall, how do you feel about your efforts with CoupleCARE? Chances are, you'll feel like you've done a pretty good job (maybe not excellent, but pretty good). Even if you feel you could have put in more effort, do not punish yourself for that. It is important to spend time thinking about the things you have done well. Allow yourself to feel good about the gains you have made as you worked through CoupleCARE.

The same principle of being kind to yourself holds for the way you manage your relationship. Nobody is kind, attentive, supportive and effective at communication all the time. What matters is putting in some effort from time to time. Perfect relationships do not exist. But truly wonderful relationships do. You have been working to make your relationship as good as you can.

So, every time you think to yourself that you've done okay, let yourself feel good for a few minutes. This is an important way of rewarding yourself for your effort.

A Final Word

In CoupleCARE we have covered many relationship skills. Our aim is to help you achieve your hopes for your relationship.

By working through the program, you've shown your commitment to moving towards your relationship goals. Congratulations for putting your time, energy and heart into it.

Thanks for sharing yourselves with us, and allowing us to share our ideas with you. We wish you the best for a long, happy, loving relationship: a love for life.

Kim Halford
for the CoupleCARE team

www.ingramcontent.com/pod-product-compliance
Lightning Source LLC
Chambersburg PA
CBHW080617270326
41928CB00016B/3101